The Polk Street Review

a celebration of Noblesville, IN

2020 edition

Sunrise

CEArts Press

a division of
CEArts, Inc.
a 501c3 nonprofit Arts organization

First Printing: 2020

Cover design: Alys Caviness-Gober
Cover art: *Sunrise Along The White River* by Alys Caviness-Gober
Project design, formatting, and layout: Alys Caviness-Gober
Editors: Alys Caviness-Gober & Sarah E. Morin

ISBN-13: 978-0-9998858-3-3

Community • Education • Arts Press
a division of *Community • Education • Arts, Inc.*
Noblesville, IN 46060
1st Printing: February 2020
https://CEArts.org

Ordering Information:
Special discounts are available on quantity purchases by corporations, associations, educators, and others. Please contact Alys at info@cearts.org for details.
U.S. trade bookstores and wholesalers: please contact Alys at info@cearts.org for details.

*Dedicated to
our community,
our friends,
and
our families*

2020 *Community • Education • Arts, Inc.* Acknowledgements

Community • Education • Arts, Inc. (CEArts) is the grateful recipient of an arts project support grant for the 2020 edition of *The Polk Street Review* from the Indiana Arts Commission. CEArts is a vital part of the Noblesville Cultural Arts District, and partners with the Noblesville Cultural Arts Council and Nickel Plate Arts. This book, and everything we do, would not be possible without the help of these wonderful organizations.

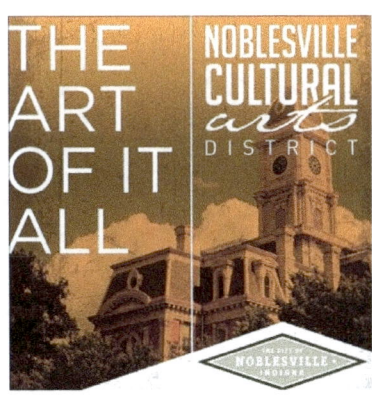

The Polk Street Review 2020 Corporate Sponsors

Community • Education • Arts, Inc. gratefully thanks the following local businesses for their support of the 2020 edition of *The Polk Street Review*. We hope you will give them your business!

Martin & Martin
Insurance Agency
#HEREFORYOU

62 S. 9th Street
Noblesville, IN 46060
www.martinandmartin.biz
PH: 773.3743 TXT: 317.674.3173

Erie Insurance®

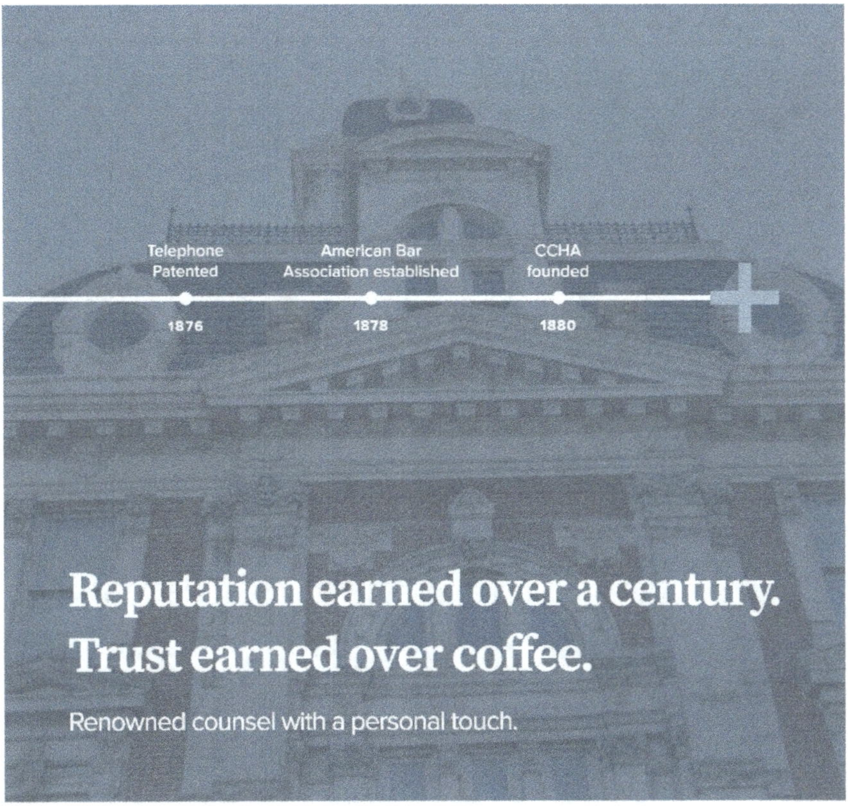

Table of Contents:

Introduction

About Polk Street (the actual street!), Ants & Grasshoppers, and *Community • Education • Arts, Inc.*

The Polk Street Review book is named in honor of a significant and historic Noblesville street. When Noblesville was laid out in 1823, the north/south road that eventually had railroad tracks running alongside and down the middle of it was named after William Connor's partner, Josiah Polk. It is now called 8th Street.

Polk Street was a busy road: mills were at the north end, and the old courthouse, bars, liveries, hotels, homes, and other buildings of industry lined its southern stretch. At some point in Noblesville's history, Polk Street/8th Street became the dividing line between white-collar and blue-collar neighborhoods, white and African American neighborhoods, residential and industrial areas, and high ground *versus* the flood plain. Over time, those distinctions became so ingrained that people didn't even mentioned them; now most folks just see 8th Street as what it originally was: a main route through town. The busy street, like history itself, can be taken for granted, but it represents the history of Noblesville, her businesses, and the generations of people who have lived here.

Unfortunately, the tracks and the trains that ran on them until just a few years ago have been removed. Noblesville has seen its heritage railway train tracks vanish as developers had their way, but Noblesville residents who honor and celebrate their city's history will forever keep the historic tracks and trains in their hearts. They'll continue to believe that Noblesville can retain the historic small-town qualities that make it unique from its neighbors, and still honor its history as a place of growth and development.

Certain areas, certain landmarks, and certain streets play a big part in that vision. The railroad tracks in and along Noblesville's old Polk Street were a good example of what shaped Noblesville in the past, and what made Noblesville always feel special. In today's developer-driven world, Noblesville must look to the future and hope that it can remain a special place with a small-town feel.

As we go to print with this edition of our annual anthology, we're not sure that all of the city's changes and developments are good for Noblesville in the long run. Amid these changes, we're reminded of our theme this year, *Sunrise*, and we must have faith that the residents of Noblesville, the old families who've been here for generations and the new ones more dedicated to development and change, can find a way to greet each sunrise together, and protect Noblesville's unique atmosphere. We're doing what we can, as a small nonprofit organization, to keep Noblesville's heart and soul alive. Using the name Polk Street in our anthology's title is one way we honor our city's heritage.

The Polk Street Review's purpose is to capture and celebrate that heritage and history, and the people who live and work here (past and present!), in submissions of prose, poetry, song lyrics, and images. We ask that either the subject matter in a submission or the submitter have a connection to Noblesville, but that old "rule" is getting harder and harder to enforce, as our organization grows globally and we receive quality submissions from faraway places.

You may have heard us refer to our *The Polk Street Review* contributors as *grasshoppers* and to the people who quietly support them as *ants.* These insect references are taken from Aesop's fable, *The Ant & The Grasshopper*. Grasshoppers are the dreamers, the creatives: the artists, writers, and musicians among us. Ants are the ones who support them: the hardworking loved ones toiling away in the background, the ones who handle the realities of life. Grasshoppers create that which inspires, that which feeds the soul; ants create that which feeds the body. The world needs both ants and grasshoppers, so cheers to both!

Community • Education • Arts, Inc. (CEArts) is a 501(c)(3) nonprofit Arts organization that is based in Noblesville with a global reach. Our organization is run by a small band of dedicated people volunteering time out of their busy lives to keep our nonprofit alive. Many of you know that *Community • Education • Arts* was legally called *Logan Street Sanctuary*, and that we rebranded our 501(c)(3) in 2019 when the property that we had rented for over five years sold. As we scrambled to update anything and everything that carried our name online (*ie*, create a new website, update social media accounts, grants accounts, inform partner organizations, *etc*), move out all of our belongings, and salvage as many of our projects and events as we could, we quickly realized that not having our own space would force us to innovate to continue to do the things we love to do.

The Things We Love To Do

Embracing an organizational rebranding process is neither a simple nor an easy thing to do, and there were plenty of dark days and nights before our organization's *Sunrise* dawned hopeful!

By the way, this is the first year we asked for public input for this edition's theme: we had a Theme Contest, and *Sunrise* won ~ Congratulations, Deborah Petersen, who submitted the winning theme! As we chose the winning theme, CEArts President Alys Caviness-Gober was reminded of when she was a very ill child and living through the night was not a guarantee. Alys has never taken for granted the dawning of a new day.

With the *Sunrise* theme in mind, we felt submissions could relate to new beginnings, fresh starts, light-bulb moments, clarity, firsts, removals, ends of depression and times of darkness, finding brilliance, blessings, understanding, timelessness, and so many other things. Also to celebrate and represent our organizational changes, we've opted to depart from our traditional black and white cover design for this edition of *The Polk Street Review* ~ we hope you like this year's cover!

Our organization has met our rebranding challenges head-on, finding different venues around town for workshops and our annual *NICE*

(Noblesville Interdisciplinary Creativity Expo) presentations event and *The Polk Street Review* (TPSR) book launch. A big thank you to the Hamilton County Artists' Association for letting us host this year's book launch in their historic and lovely *Birdie Gallery*!

We've also come up with some innovative options to expand opportunities for artists, musicians, and writers. We've added a lot of digital content to our repertoire, like our *@theroundtable* podcast and arts-related short videos series, and online *Arts Showcase* opportunities for artists, writers, and musicians to exhibit their work 24/7 online. We've been busy!

Thank you to our 2020 volunteers for all their hard work!

2020 CEArts Volunteers

Board Officers:
President: Alys Caviness-Gober
Secretary: Sarah E. Morin
Treasurer: Joyce Perry

CEArts Irregulars (our intrepid volunteers):
Cris Gober
Emily Wasonga
James Weston

2020 Sunrise by Alys Caviness-Gober

As I begin writing this personal introductory essay for the 2020 edition of *The Polk Street Review*, it is a mild winter pre-dawn morning in early December 2019. In years past, I start to work on the layout and formatting of this annual publication on 01 January, immediately following the annual December 31 submissions deadline. This year, I'm getting a jump-start on things like designing the book cover, title page, front matter, this essay ~ anything I can do before that 31 December deadline. *Why*, you ask? Well, let me tell you! It's a little story that works perfectly with our 2020 theme, *Sunrise*.

Before I tell you my little story, a little background about our publishing process. Our print deadline for *The Polk Street Review* is 01 February each year. In early January, my arts-partner Sarah E. Morin and I go through submissions and select and edit the ones to publish. Then we choose our award winners, and by mid-January I'm compiling a manuscript draft in a Word document. That draft goes to Sarah E. for her final proofread. Here is where I must say: *any and all remaining typos and errors in this book are mea culpa!*

After Sarah E.'s final proofing, I create my working draft, which goes through what feels like a million and one permutations. For past editions, I'm on my computer 12-14 hours a day every day in January, editing, formatting, *etc* ~ to catch typos and misspellings that we missed or that Word's spellchecker won't "see" because it recognizes that both *and* and *an* are spelled correctly even when one or the other is contextually incorrect. At some point, I say, *Enough!*

Then, my publishing work begins: formatting and laying out the book to fit our 6x9 print size. Again, it seems like I create a million and one permutations of drafts before I have "the one" ready for the printer.

Such are my January days and nights every year since we started publishing *The Polk Street Review* four years ago. Yes, friends, the 2020 edition of *The Polk Street Review* is the fourth one we've published!

Now, my personal little story starts in late February of 2019. Two days after the 2019 edition's 23 February book launch, I was hospitalized for 15 days. I was both exhausted and again battling *pew-moan-ya* (my lung disease manifests as repeated pneumonias). Being hospitalized is no fun, but those of you who know me, know that my disabilities make hospitalizations and other medical treatments routine.

The timing was poor: my daughter and her husband were expecting their first child, a boy, at the end of March (he is the first grandchild for both sides of his family!). I planned to help with the baby as much as needed, so as long I was healthier and out of the hospital before our grandchild was born, I was okay with being hospitalized for a couple weeks.

On the last evening of my hospitalization, I was anxiously awaiting being discharged the next evening. The grueling schedule of IV antibiotics coursing into me 6 times in every 24-hours at a 3-hour drip rate (leaving only about 1 hour between doses), coupled with enduring *two* bronchoscopies within three days, might be hard to imagine, but suffice to say I was *more than ready* to go home.

It was late in the evening that night, around 10:30PM. Cris was half-asleep in an uncomfortable hospital chair when I got a text message from our son-in-law ~ they were two floors down in maternity! It was 10 days before the due date, but . . . that baby was coming!

I may or may not have shrieked aloud, which startled Cris from his dozing, and rang for the nurses, begging them to roll me down to maternity so that I could see my daughter before delivery. The nurses were awesome ~ I think they were as excited as I was ~ and as soon as my current drip ended, they trundled me into a wheelchair and rolled me down to maternity.

I can't describe the moment I saw *my* baby girl as she prepared to meet her own little baby. Who can describe that feeling? It is poignant, tear-filled, joyous, terrifying, overwhelming, and so much more.

Throughout the night, our son-in-law kept us informed. Cris stayed at the hospital. My IV antibiotic schedule continued. My nurses rolled me down to maternity between every dose; Cris and I hung out in the maternity hallways ~ just being close was all we could "do." Then Cris'd roll me back up for another 3-hour drip.

A little before 12 noon the next day (my discharge day!), as we were leaving to go back up to my room for the next IV dose, the maternity nurses told us that the baby wouldn't be born for a few more hours.

Okay perfect timing, I thought, *we won't miss anything ~ he'll be born right around the time this next three-hour drip ends, and we'll come back down and we shall meet him!*

About 20 minutes into that noon dose, our son-in-law sent me a little video: it was my daughter, holding her just-born son.

Words fail me; suffice to say, I couldn't really focus on anything other than that little video. Mother and baby, safe and sound. Sigh of delight.

Man, waiting for that drip to finish was the LONGEST three hours!

But it did finally end, and Cris and I whisked downstairs at wheelchair-breakneck speed to shower all of our love upon "our kids" and their brand-new baby.

Is there anything better than the birth of a baby? A brand-new life enters our world! It's like the entire Universe dawns anew, reborn in a split second, and everything beautiful and possible and loving and kind and sweet soars aloft and fills the very air.

In *Gone With The Wind*, Miss Melly says, *the happiest days are when babies come*.

I say, *Amen, Miss Melly*.

I remember saying, at some point that first day, to my daughter: *Who but me would be two floors up in the same hospital on the day their first grandchild is born?!* And she replied, *Well, at least you were close!* And close I shall stay, forever.

Cris and I went back down to see them between all of my IV doses that day; safe to say, we were already *addicted-to-love* for that little baby!

Hospital-bedhead-hair me, meeting my grandson.

I was discharged around 10PM that night, the first day of our grandson's life. Bright and early the next morning, wearing a mask to protect my compromised immune system, I was back at the hospital to visit! I've been happily helping out with our grandson ever since, almost daily.

I offer you this little story as an explanation as to how my life now, with a grandchild, fits our theme this year, *Sunrise*. A new day has dawned for me, and life has definitely changed! That's why I'm working early, in December, on anything I can for this edition ~ because my weekdays this year revolve around taking care of our grandson.

Because of everything I've already told you, this book would not exist without the help, support, encouragement, and love that I receive from four people: first, my wonderful ant-husband, Cris, and my dear grasshopper/ant-friend Sarah E. Morin. I can't ever thank them enough, but . . . *thank you both!* And second, *thank you* to my son and my daughter for their love, support, and understanding of my creative craziness! I'm so happy that both my son and my son-in-law contributed pieces to this year's *The Polk Street Review*.

This edition's *Sunrise* theme brought in absolutely amazing pieces: poignant, hilarious, sobering, thought-provoking ~ we have it all, as people looked back, reflected on the past, imagined the future, evaluated lessons learned, or just plain told a good story through word or image.

About the *Awards* (you'll find them listed near the end of the book). Selecting award winners is always a tough job, and this year was no exception. Sarah E. and I truly believe that every single piece in this book deserves to be recognized, but *1*) no one closely related to anyone on the *CEArts* Board is eligible for awards, and *2*) we just can't give out awards to everyone.

The awards for our three categories, *Prose, Song Lyrics & Poetry*, and *Images*, are: *First Place, Second Place, Third Place*, and one *Honorable Mention*.

This year, for the first time, and each year from now on, we have a *Grand Prize* ribbon award for our annual *Theme Contest* winner, who also receives two complimentary books.

We have two *Special Awards* this year: *Special Awards* are given in recognition of something that's kind of hard to put into words. *Special Awards* recognize not one particular piece of writing or imagery, but rather one submitter. No matter how many pieces he or she submitted, a *Special Award* goes to a person whose submission(s) are at a level of excellence that shows us the person is somehow just a bit distinct than the norm: perhaps taking a risk (in life or art form), has a fresh perspective or voice, or has submitted piece/pieces that are somehow different than most of the submissions we receive. It's exciting to have two *Special Award* winners this year!

The Polk Street Review's highest honor is the *Award of Merit*, which we've nicknamed *Best in Book*. The *Award of Merit* recognizes one submission from any of the three categories that hits our *trifecta*: it is technically and artistically outstanding, meets our guidelines, and elicits an emotionally connective reaction. The *Award of Merit* piece is one that is felt deeply for a long time, in your heart and soul.

Selecting the *Award of Merit* winner, and all the other awards winners, is both fun and challenging for us. We hope you'll appreciate our awards selections this year.

On a personal note, I hope you enjoy reading the 2020 edition as much as I enjoyed putting it together! The past year was one of challenges for many of our TPSR grasshoppers and ants. It certainly was for me personally, and for our organization, and I for one am happy to embrace with joyful anticipation each and every *Sunrise* that come my way!

Alys Caviness-Gober
President
Community • Education • Arts, Inc.

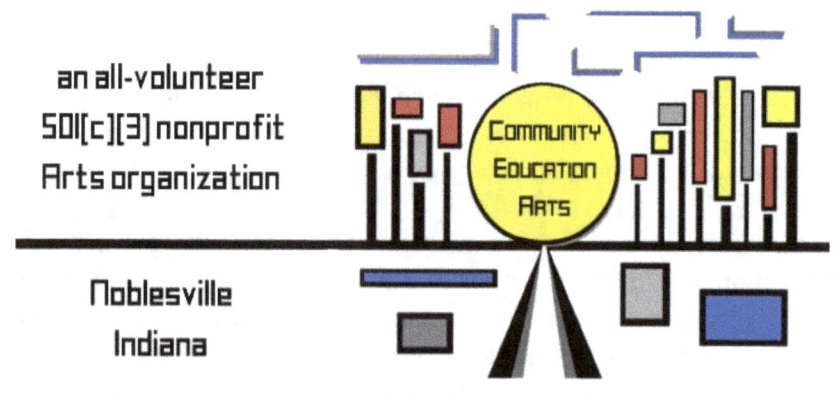

an all-volunteer
501[c][3] nonprofit
Arts organization

Community
Education
Arts

Noblesville
Indiana

Macwood by Sarah E. Morin

Holy Morning by Sarah E. Morin

I wake before my alarm.
God shook my shoulder.

I don a pilgrim's hood, my grey sweatshirt.
He calls me outside

into the monochrome edge of the day
just before dawn opens her eyes.

The world catches and holds her breath.
I exhale incense into the chilly air.

My dew-baptized feet
dance to bring forth the sun.

My pleading fingers split the rays,
comb them through my hair.

Supplicant and celebrant, I
plow my prayers into deep rows of earth.

The fields my spacious sanctuary.
The birds my chorus of praise.

The sky a high-vaulted cathedral
refracting stained-glass light.

The golden stubble of cornstalks
form an amber mosaic of resurrection.

My soul is a universe, expanding ever faster
across my ancestors' farmland.

Stretch out to embrace everything that is,
everything the light touches.

This morning, before I am small again,
I am made holy

Nothing can contain me.
I taste infinite God.

True Romance by Evan Dossey

And till this day, the events that followed all still seems like a distant dream. But the dream was real and was to change our lives forever. I kept asking Clarence why our world seemed to be collapsing and things seemed to be getting so shitty. And he'd say, "That's the way it goes. But don't forget, it goes the other way, too." That's the way romance is ... Usually, that's the way it goes. But every once in a while, it goes the other way, too.

You're So Cool, You're So Cool, You're So Cool.

I was introduced to the film *True Romance*[1] through the happenstance of my dad owning the soundtrack, which I found and added to my Winamp library back in 2002 while preparing for a family road trip to – I think? – South Carolina. While making the mix, I happened upon

---

[1] True Romance (1993) https://www.imdb.com/title/tt0108399/

You're So Cool, the film's theme, a Hans Zimmer composition that borrows pretty heavily from Carl Orff's *Gassenhauer*, as heard in Terrence Malick's *Badlands*.

It played endlessly on my Walkman during that trip. In fact, I don't really remember anything about that trip besides *You're So Cool*. It became my private anthem of sorts over the years, the song I would listen to, to fall asleep in any environment, anywhere – camping trips with Boy Scouts, family trips, the school bus, at work. Alaska. I didn't actually *watch True Romance* for another three years, but when I did, I fell deeply in love with it.

Quentin Tarantino sold the *True Romance* script to fund his debut film, *Reservoir Dogs*, a much darker movie. In truth, Tarantino's original script for *True Romance* was much darker, too, until director Tony Scott flipped a few acts around and saved Clarence's life during the final shootout. It's otherwise vintage Tarantino – characters talk like they're much cooler than they are, women characters fend for themselves, criminals talk about movies and make wild monologues. The cast – led by Christian Slater and Patricia Arquette as lovebirds Clarence and Alabama – is more notable for its massive list of cameos: Dennis Hopper, Val Kilmer, Gary Oldman, Christopher Walken, Brad Pitt (in what may well be his quintessential role), Saul Rubinek, Bronson Pinchot, James Gandolfini, Michael Rapaport. Good shit.

Of course, watching *True Romance* in mid-2005, it never really occurred to me that this was a stacked cast. All I cared about was the way in which Tarantino heightened the relationship between Clarence and Alabama, star-crossed lovers in decaying Detroit who meet when call girl Alabama is sent by her pimp to sleep with comic-shop worker Clarence on his birthday. She meets Clarence at a Sonny Chiba triple feature by spilling popcorn on him; he's oblivious to her come-ons and is just happy to have someone with whom to enjoy the movies. They meet-cute. They fall in love. And when Clarence tries to free her from her profession, he ends up accidentally murdering her pimp and making off with a suitcase full of cocaine. Oops. The two decide to sell out in Los Angeles.

From afar, *True Romance* seems like *just* the fantasy of a teenage boy writing about what he wants from a relationship. Sure it is. But what sets it apart is how *honest* it nonetheless feels – particularly for a movie written by Quentin Tarantino. In the director's commentary, he states that people often ask if he'll make a romance movie and he says, "Well, I wrote *True Romance*." Beneath the obvious elements of "comic-shop kid meets call girl who falls in love with him, *etc. etc. etc.*," the relationship between Clarence and Alabama is always mutual, never lopsided, and the two care for one another without question in every situation.

The fantasy of *True Romance* is about two people who recognize another of their kind, and who want to love and be loved in return.

True Romance never struck me as a movie to *emulate, per se*. I guess the general fear you see online is that some people will see a violent fantasy movie and think it inspires the worst possible outcomes. Although I had not experienced my own true romance at the time, what the movie has always left me wasn't the desire to wear Elvis glasses or Hawaiian shirts or sell a bunch of coke to a producer, and it wasn't an impression that women existed to be just like Alabama.

Of all the movies about young men falling in love, *True Romance* has always felt like one of the most emotionally authentic. Not from its titillating depiction of violence and sex but from the relationship that develops between its lead characters. The romantic notion that maybe you'll meet someone just for you.

Before I met Aly in June 2013, I had only ever had two girlfriends. Those relationships didn't go so well. I still went on dates. But like any introverted and, uh, sensitive teenage boy, those didn't work out. It's ok. Dating is designed for failure. It didn't matter. I spent my time on the internet instead, mostly making shit up.

Aly was working at a comic store and I was working in a bookstore. Our first meeting was thanks to a mutual friend who was hosting an online comic-book course with Aly as her teaching assistant. I'd gone up to visit that class and the three of us went out to lunch. Aly did not seem remotely interested in talking to me . . . she was going to see *Iron Man 3* at midnight that night, with a friend she was dragging along for company. Later I slid into Aly's DMs on Twitter and told her we should go to some bookstores together. Noncommittal. So, later, I invited her to see *Man of Steel*. Hardly Sonny Chiba. Our after-movie coffee bore little resemblance to the classic scene where Clarence and Alabama go through the *Playboy* "about me" questionnaire, but I did drop my (empty) cup on the floor a few times while nervously playing with it. We bonded over Guy Pearce and his movies.

A little while later she invited me to see *Django Unchained*, which was playing again at Castleton. The next day we went to a *Star Wars* exhibit at the Indiana State Museum. Afterwards we got coffee at a cafe near where we would buy our first house five years later, and during that date she told me about how she spent her teenage years online, making shit up.

There are moments when you *know*, and that was one of them.

The first time I ever visited her we watched *Fright Night*; the first time I ever cared for her while she was sick, we watched *The Omen*. The first time she spent the night at my apartment we watched *Red Dragon*, which we still disagree about but was relevant because of our bonding over the show *Hannibal*. Most importantly, by the end of that summer we had bonded over a mutual love of *True Romance*.

It feels like a distant dream. But the dream was real and was to change our lives forever. Three years after that – and three years ago *today*[2] – *You're So Cool* played during our wedding, when we kissed as a married couple for the first time.

---

[2] originally published 16 October 2019, https://midwestfilmjournal.com/

Clear Lake Sky by Leslie Ober

Awash by Deborah Petersen

Dream drunk
Ecstatic breath life force
Unencumbered

Now,
With these rays
With this promise
The darkness ends
The fears shatter and flow away
The disillusion and pain
Under a starless night and
Without the safety of the moon
Have fallen into a colorless abyss
Now that the sun has risen.

Behold!

This paean
   This reveille
      This promise
         This breath
            This next new step
               Face up to the sky
                  To be bathed in
                     This morning brilliance.

The Pivot by Vivianne Belle

I can't remember not knowing you.

Factually, intellectually, I know there was a time before we met, but when was it? Where is it now? Time is funky, fluid, eternal. It folds, it bends, it compresses, it expands, it's everywhere and in everything all the time (oh that's *punny*). I can't see time, but I feel it. I breath it in, it scrapes through my lungs like a California wildfire.

You're in there somewhere.

Like the fabled mists of time, meeting you is so far back in my memory or my consciousness that I can't find it, I can't see it, I can't feel it; it is somewhere in a void of nonexistence that exists forever. An eternal moment.

I wish it wasn't so.

I wish I could go back to the me that was, before you. Before *you* in my life.

Now, today, it seems unfair that I can't remember me before you. I remember so much, why not *that*?

Things I do remember, the things you did; they still live within me:

The Slow Isolation.
Cutting Words.
Silences.
Bruises.
Invasion.
Assaults.
(it's still so hard to say the word *rape*)
Destruction.
Fires burning my treasures.
Fractures.
Broken teeth.
Fear.
Soul Annihilation.

I also remember what I did:

Hurt.
Cry alone.
Never tell.
Exist in fear.
      (not "live in fear": there was no living)
and then
Escape.
      (that was *The Pivot*)

It took a long time to get away.
I had nothing. I had nowhere. I went anyway.
It was go . . . or die.

They call it *recovery*, I guess, or *PTSD*. Although *PTSD* is ongoing, so maybe that dark downward time trying to climb up back to something that felt like *me* wasn't PTSD but rather something else. Maybe *recovery*. But *recovery* associates with *addiction*, right? I wasn't addicted to you.

I was imprisoned *by you*.

I escaped.
(that was *The Pivot*)

The Pivot took me down down down into a darkness unimaginable and also lost in the mists of time.

When I turned away from you, I faced that darkness. I turned away from you to save myself. Or rather, what was left of my *self*. I had to face such bleakness. *Processing*, they call it. I call it staring stoically into the face of *it*. Staring into the face of *me* – of the me I had become, facing the grief for the me I had lost, facing of the fear of the me that was yet to be.

I'm not sure what to call the time after *The Pivot*, after my escape: maybe even that time, that part of my life, is so fluid, so funky, so eternal it is still here now within me. Still now today, that dark journey folds, it bends, it compresses, it expands, it's everywhere and in everything all the time.

Because even *Escape* never ends.

Each day when I awaken, you're with me. As I walk these halls, as I drive these roads, as I see and greet and talk to familiar friendly faces, you're with me. As I lay down my head at night, you're with me. Always, in my dreaming and my nightmares, you're with me.

I wish I could remember not knowing you.

Sunrise by Marlene Million
(after Monet's *Impression, Sunrise* 1872)

The pre-dawn hush heralds promise
of your presence. You whisper
"good-night" to sister moon.
Morning haze hovers over
your reflection, mirrored a dusty orange.

Your tip of brightness shimmers,
sparkles a zig-zag path atop water.
The Harbor, misty with dew,
blurs with shyness. The sky cradles
buoyant energy at your command.

Master of ceremonies, such humble
regard awaits your rising. Ships' masts,
dockside cranes, your captive audience,
pay homage. Factories and ships
stand as sentinels in respect.

The anchor pulls free, and a vessel
floats towards the horizon,
guided by your faint light.
There is pause . . .

when you touch the heart of day!

Summer Lake Sunrise by Leslie Ober

The Night Bobby Came to the Mall by Sandy Stewart

The Coffee House

Sometime in the 1960s (I was there, so can't exactly remember), I visited a coffee house in Bloomington, Indiana and fell madly in lust. Having felt like an alien being on the wrong planet for most of my life, I thought I had finally reached the mother ship! The Hippy movement wasn't just a fashion statement in those days, but a coming together and rising-up of dissatisfied, disillusioned youth raised under the threat of nuclear annihilation. We suspected that the "duck and cover" drills we had practiced would not protect us since they were concocted and executed by the very adults who had fucked up our world. *Never trust anyone over thirty!* we cried with one voice. (To our great surprise, we eventually became thirty, forty, fifty, and so on until "live fast, die young and leave a beautiful corpse" was no longer an option).

But back then, we were determined to undo our parents' mistakes, even though considerably hampered by the fact that approximately 50% of us could be drafted any time to potentially die in a truly unholy war. We protested that war, burned draft cards, chased deferments, moved to Canada, harbored fugitives, and stuck flowers in gun barrels – determined to unite this fractured world in peace and love. Of course, we all know how that worked out! But it was a valiant and beautiful effort, gently executed by lovely flower children drifting along in a purple haze. This is the story of just such a haze.

When I entered the Coffee House that fateful sixties night, the performer on stage was everything I dreamed of and absolutely nothing I needed. He had scruffy long hair and a beard (a mark of authenticity and true commitment, as not everyone in the new movement had yet had time to sprout) and was playing his guitar Delta Blues bottle neck style while wailing a Sleepy John Estes lament about the dearth of "deep-sea diving women." Seems there were just none "to be found." *I'm a deep-sea diving woman*, I instantly decided.

I went home with Mr. Delta Blues that night and married him two weeks later. I married him for two excellent reasons. One: because my parents threw him out of the house when I brought him home to Noblesville for a visit. Two: I had just broken an engagement to a very nice boy simply because I was restless and bored. So, I thought that I should just dive head-first into this relationship before the inevitable *ennui* set in. As the nice boy was the third young man I had planned to marry and didn't, I was beginning to think I might be too damaged and fickle to truly commit. So I just plunged into that marriage without pausing to check the depth. It worked out pretty much as you might imagine, but I learned a bunch of useful stuff. For example, just because a man sings about it doesn't mean he really wants a deep-sea diving woman. A shallow woman that can tread water is more than enough for most, and a sassy drowning woman is way too much.

I'm a little fuzzy on details and timeline, but during the tumultuous year of our short marriage, Mr. Blues and I left the Bloomington campus and ended up in New Albany, Indiana for a semester. I worked for the census bureau and took evening classes at the Indiana University Jeffersonville extension.

Bobby and the purple haze, March 24, 1968

Shortly before I was to leave for my Anthropology class at IU's Jeffersonville campus, a Bloomington friend dropped by and passed around a truly epic joint. I'm still not entirely sure what the three of us smoked, but as soon as I got into my car and hit the interstate, I knew I should have declined. I still remember that the exit ramp to campus felt a bit like Alice's tumble down the rabbit hole. It seemed to spiral on forever! (Fairly vivid flashbacks still occur from time to time when I'm on a curved ramp like that one). That night, I was certain I would never reach the end. I know I prayed a lot – *just let me get off this ramp and into my class and I'll never toke and drive again!*

I reached my class on time and am pleased to report that I have kept that promise, at least. That night, each step I took on the way to class was perilous, but I focused on the end goal. Just hold it together long enough to walk into the room and sit down at my desk. (Prayer was involved with this journey, as well). The floor was tilting and reeling, though I might have appeared nearly normal as I navigated the space – clutching other desks for balance until I reached my front row seat and heaved a great sigh of relief because I was safe for the next two hours and would likely come back to earth by the end of class.

"Good evening," said the handsome young professor. "Robert Kennedy is speaking at the Youngstown Shopping Mall in Jeffersonville tonight."

He then announced that Anthropology class that evening would be a field trip to hear the great man speak. As I tried to absorb this news while grappling with the fact that I might have to leave my safe seat and manage to walk erect, he said, "Raise your hand if you drove here tonight."

You would think I would have kept still, but you would be wrong. I fought through the fog and raised my hand. "I have a car," is what I think I said. The professor then organized a carpool by dividing class members and assigning each to a vehicle – all except mine. Starting to feel a little relief, I then heard my professor say, "I'll ride with you."

Once we reached the car, I managed to start it, shift into gear, and begin the drive. My professor shifted, as well, and placed his hand on my leg. Gob-smacked and dumbstruck for a moment, I finally bleated, "I'm married." And, that's all I remember until we reached the mall.

I sort of heard the great man speak, and history records that it was a great speech, addressing serious issues important to me at the time, such as Viet Nam and Civil Rights. Sadly, the only thing I remember was Bobby saying we should vote for him because he had a lot of children to support and needed the job. That snapped me out of my stupor! I was furious! How dare he joke when our world was in shambles. (Did I mention that I took myself quite seriously in those days?) I didn't think our perilous future was any laughing matter. Sadly, I had no capacity then to appreciate the kind of man who could make jokes and continue the struggle after having survived the hellish loss of his beloved brother. Now I am amazed at his strength! How could he keep fighting? How could he laugh and carry on? Why didn't he tell us the truth about why he wanted to be our next president? My heart was bleeding, and I wanted truth!

Of course, he may have done so – and brilliantly. He may have soothed all our bleeding hearts. I just missed it because I was stoned. Maybe that's the night Bobby declared, "Some men see things as they are and say, *Why?* I dream of things that never were and say, *Why not?*" I know that this great man managed to quell a potential riot and calm an angry grieving crowd in Indianapolis just eleven days later when Dr. King was assassinated. How did he muster the strength, wisdom, and determination to carry on? Because he truly was a great man, and I missed appreciating him because I was a foolish little girl.

By the way, I encountered the handsome young professor a year or so later at a "love in" on the Bloomington campus. Bobby was dead; and my first choice for president, Eugene McCarthy, had lost heart and dropped out of the race. My world had darkened considerably, but I was single again! (Who saw that coming?) The professor was looking a little shopworn – neither as young nor as handsome as I remembered. We hugged, danced a little, and then I floated far, far away – to the isle of Manhattan, where I encountered unlimited opportunities to practice deep sea diving, with the occasional drowning and resuscitation. Eventually, I washed ashore in Noblesville where I found a genuine, bonified deep-sea diving, guitar pickin' man! Turns out he was there all the time.

Blue City by Simona Buna

The First Dawn by George W. Wolfe
(for my daughter Esther)

She awakens at 6AM, less
than seven months old, reaching
for the goldfinch that flew
out of her dream. There she lies
laughing with the sun, as if
to know creation's riddle. She
never feels funny about clapping
with one hand.

We stroll to the convenience
store where her smile is
heard above the radio. Even the
caffeine-faced clerk responds,
thawing his lips enough to
break up the freeze-dried look
in his eyes.

Life is simple now. No shoes to tie
or teeth to brush, no sins to
repent or dualities to wrestle.
Day and night are but theaters for
different dreams, personal identity
an enduring myth.

"I am everything . . ."
she exclaims with featherweight eyes.

But today something has changed. Now
she looks, still smiles, but
sees the distance between us.

Lover's Rest by Jess Coovert

I wonder if there will ever be a day I stop loving you.
When I'd come home, work weary and exhausted,
Only to see you left your towel on the bathroom floor

In a wet puddle. I would pick and hang it up to dry,
Smiling to myself as I stumbled to our bedroom to
See you curled up in the sheets with your hair a wild mess.
And drool caked on your cheeks in the perfect display
Of uncharacteristic realness.

The Joy of Dawn by Sarah E. Morin

The first thing I do when I rise
before I eat or exercise
is fill the deep sink in my kitchen
to wash every last dirty dish in.

Some folk wake to chirping birds,
but the most useful sounds I've heard
to stir sluggish blood in sleepy veins
are running faucets and glugging drains.

Steam drawn into icy nose,
the heat seeps down to slippered toes.
At once, cold fingers scour and scrub
and luxuriate in a private hot tub.

I bathe my stiff hands like a prayer,
each coffee mug with tender care
and let the frothy lemon bubbles
soak away yesterday's troubles.

Pale rays spill through kitchen window
in a yellow-rose crescendo.
The sun rises, I'm bathed in light.
Warmth chases away the chill of night.

The best part of waking up
is stacking plates and bowls and cups.
The reasoned, regimental lines
straighten chaos in my mind.

Blank countertop a fresh new slate
to write my day. I anticipate
as the sun floats on pastel horizon
the Joy of rising with the Dawn.

Lake House Dreams by Leslie Ober

Dawn by Vivianne Belle

Dawn is daily born in a myriad of yellows and peaches and pinks and lavenders; her colors slide up into the dark night's sky with both form and function, purpose and ease. *Her colors*, I said, because she seems to be a woman, at least by our culturally-defined religion-commanded gender-related color norms (and ancient Greco-Roman tradition). In the Spring, she springs up bursting with energetic frenzy, sweeping away the pre-sunrise fogs and the dying Winter's last clouds as if she carries before her a witch's broom. Her awakening on a Summer morn is slow, she stretches out her long warm wiggling golden fingers as if to tickle away the dank and cloying humid night air. Her spirit wanes a bit in the Fall, and she awakes with a cool sigh, knowing her strength, like that of our older selves, is starting to fade; her colors are a little less intense, her reach into the dark sky is a little less far. She yawns most sleepily at daybreak in Winter. Like the rest of us unwilling to arise into the cold dark air, she resists leaving the warm confines of her bedding among the nighttime stars. Dawn is daily born; she is like a magician, waving across our world her magical scarves of ever-changing tints and shades and tones of yellows and peaches and pinks and lavenders.

Good Morning by David Allen

Good morning
I awake and kiss you lightly on the cheek
    (your pillow is bare)
And softly stroke your long, brown hair.
You turn in bed to face me
Looking into my eyes with eyes
I love to drown my soul in
    (there's but one body's impression
there's but one side of the bed to make).

I whisper softly that I love you
The radio answers with a song
    (I leave it playing all night long
      to accompany this loneliness).

I start to leave; you reach for my hand,
We touch
    (the air is not as soft)
You pull me to your side
    (I stare at the pillow)
I take your head in my hands
We kiss,
Wine sweet.

The taste turns bitter
You slowly dissolve
Parts of you breaking apart
A jigsaw puzzle
I scream
I pick up the pieces of you
And start to glue
But the head's on backwards.

My dog jumps on the bed
Scattering you around the room
On my knees I search for you
My dog licks my face
My eyes lose their sleep
I awake.

There is no puzzle
My dog sleeps, head nuzzled
In the crook of my arm
You are at home
Unaware that for a while
We made love in
The life of my night.

Remnants by Jenny Kalahar

At the end, full of water, barely bone
barely sinew
I know I will transform
into something like a sister to the clouds,

puff and white as the ghosts in Victorian sketches,
as sinister as the feeling of night
no light, no candle, no moon,
wandering a path I know
by feel, by memory, by echolocation,
my cheekbones pointed,
eyes closed and sunken
until what remains on my pillow
is nearly nothing but wetted dust.

The grandmother clock
laughing instead of ticking
cruel and irreversible
waits until the indifferent nurse leaves
waits until the black cat slinks away
waits until his youthful, aching letters
white as my skin
fall from my fingers to the floor
that callous clock waits to skim ahead to morning
where I will awaken elsewhere
finding light
finding peace
finding sisters in the clouds

Blowing Things Up by Mark Wilkinson

From a young age, boys like to "up" things. Tear up, burn up, blow up. Maybe it's hardwired into our brains, but it's always a boy who burns down his garage or bends the rim on his bicycle jumping over something.

We like it. It feels good.

Every neighborhood has the kids who always seems to possess the means to make these things happen. They have access to tools, lighters, lighter fluid, and fireworks on a regular basis. In my neighborhood it was my neighbors, Perry and Terry Conway.

The Conway clan was a tough lot. Heck and Wanda were the parents and had six kids, all of whom could beat me up. Even the dog, Rinnie, took his turn, chasing me on my bicycle and biting my leg. It was a rough and tumble family and the boys, particularly Perry and Terry, became what was known in small town parlance as "hoodlums."

Being a hoodlum did not require any great effort. You had to be able to stand sullenly on the sidewalk in front of the laundromat, swear occasionally, and smoke cigarettes. These hoodlums were my heroes and my nightmares. Their savoir-faire was immeasurable. Their command of the sidewalk total. If they deigned to speak to me then my esteem among the fearful rose like a bottle rocket. If they punched me in the arm, the honor far outweighed the pain. You were somebody.

There was definitely a yin and yang of having hoodlums for neighbors. On one side, I was always available for random beatings, torturing, and terrorizing. And I never ratted them out. Even as a kid, the code of omerta was in force. There were positives of having the Conways next door. They were always up for kick the can or football. And if the brothers were on different sides, I knew the loser would fight the winner sooner or later, and it would not be me taking a beating. Plus, they always had the good stuff. Matches, lighters, and cigarettes, punishable offenses in my house, were always available to the Conway boys. And they were master thieves at Massey's Drug Store. As far as I can remember, they never bought a candy bar or a comic book. They took what they wanted.

One of the real perks of having Perry and Terry for neighbors is that they would, in their way, look out for me. I was their thrall. They could torment, tease, torture, and terrorize me, but others had to get their permission. It worked for me. Better the devil you know, right?

Even though I was given relatively free rein to roam the streets of Shirley, Indiana at a young age, I was not what one would consider worldly. I knew *my* world: it was the corner of White and Shirley Streets. I knew what a firecracker was, but I had never seen a blasting cap. A blasting cap is a small explosive used to detonate larger explosives, such as a stick of dynamite. They were, at the time of my youth, readily available and notoriously unstable. Basically, a blasting cap was a metal tube full of black powder with a fuse. They were the real deal and could blow off fingers with their blasts and put out eyes with their metal fragments. When I was in elementary school, I had never seen one.

We walked to and from school in those days. Sometimes we cut through yards and down alleys. Sometimes, we met our friends and walked down the sidewalks. One day, I was taking the sidewalk home with my friends. As we approached an alley, I noticed something new and a little bit disconcerting. The Conway brothers were lurking in the alley. This was no surprise. They were notorious lurkers. The surprise was that they were accompanied by the Haffner bothers, Ferell and Jodie. Most small towns had multiple hoodlum families that provided generations of smokers, truants, and thieves. The Conways and the Haffners were two of ours. Normally, the progeny of these clans kept their distance from one another, since proximity seemed to ignite some primal need to assert dominance, leading to blood, bruises, and repercussions from older siblings. Today, they lurked together.

If I had been paying attention, I would have cut down New Jersey Street, but it was too late to change. I would just take my chances on a punch in the arm, a minor inconvenience. As I attempted to ease past the group, Jodie Haffner spoke to me.

"Hey, kid," he said. "Come here."

I stepped off the sidewalk into the alley.

"Hold this," he said.

I took a chunk of concrete block from him, obedient to authority as always.

"Drop it on that," he said. He pointed to a metal tube in the alley as he backed away.

I raised the concrete, ready to slam it down on the shiny object.

"Don't do it, Mark!" Terry said urgently.

I was stunned. To my knowledge, Terry, five years older than me, had never called me by my first name. He either called me kid or fartknocker. I took the last as an insult but never complained. His authority was without question, both in nicknames and behavior. I did not drop the concrete.

"That's a blasting cap," Terry said.

He assumed his explanation was enough. I gave him the concrete and backed out of the alley. I had no idea what a blasting cap was. It was years later when I realized that Terry Conway saved me from whatever maiming or blinding that this small explosive would have wrought on me. It was years after that when I realized that Jodie Haffner would have let me hurt myself severely for his own enjoyment.

This was a turning point in my relationship with my hoodlum neighbor. He cared enough about me, or the trouble he would get into, to keep me from blowing myself up. He never mentioned it to me, nor did I ever bring it up to him. I never ratted Jodie Haffner out to my parents, either, which may have been why Terry treated me better. He still called me fartknocker, but he didn't make it sound like an insult.

I never became a hoodlum, but I admired their ethos. And I have the fingers and toes to prove it.

Insomniac's Lament by Arlene Barker

Sleep . . .
Elusive guardian of dreams,
Second hand percussionist,
tick . . . tick . . . tick...
keeping time in the darkness.
The more you hide from me
the more I seek your power
over tomorrow's possibilities.

Like a petulant child
unresponsive to my pleas,
you arrive when you see fit,

leaving my weary body and
gerbil-wheel of running thoughts
desperate to be at rest, and
restored by healing slumber.

Could we call a truce?
Come to an understanding?
Remember how we used to be
such easy friends not so long ago?

Tick . . . tick . . . tick

Light begins to permeate the night.
Avian chatter announces the sunrise.
Sadly, as I write these restless words,
I realize that you have passed me by
once again.

Melodic by Jess Coovert

The sun was rising, a new day had come. Orange and pink streaked
the sky in wild paint strokes, like a God decided to dabble in
impressionism.

One, two, three, four. The stage was electric with feeling. Notes
danced off the pages in a wild tango, unakin to the rhythm inscribed
in their DNA.

One, two, three, four. It was the fourth movement of the song. Fast.
Faster than the rest. A peak, like the nights spent in the practice rooms
with Gerald, the French horn. My fingers danced across the strings,
whining out a melody in fifth and six position.

One, two, three, four. We started slow. A mournful tune that had the
audience depressed at the very first note. Low, dark, like a man
lurking down the street on a foggy night in a suit, briefcase in hand.
No one knows him or where he's going, but he has someone to meet,
an important message to tell.

One, two, three, four. I was nervous. Hands shaking in unintentional vibrato. The theatre was silent, the slightest shift or scratch of the nose could be heard as I raised my bow and began to play. A solo, quiet at first, like snow falling on your eyelashes then louder, faster, heavier, more emotional, and deep and profound.

One, two, three, four. The curtain rose; *show time*.

Midwest Sunset by Leslie Ober

Shall I? by Deborah Petersen

And, so,
What would I do for your Love?

Shall I
Color my hair,
Lose weight,
Laugh more?
Shall I
Read the books you know,
Use bigger words,
Speak of current events?
Shall I
Change my beliefs,
Reorder my values,
Don your biases?
Shall I
Climb mountains
Hike miles and miles
Swim in many oceans?
Shall I…

No.
It will be enough
To stand here and see you
To breathe you
To accept all of you
To offer all of who
I am
Right here, right now

To love you strongly
And allow myself to be loved courageously.

All of you, all of me
At no cost.

Tree Whispers by Dennis L. White

You whisper through curling yellowed parchment
And faded photos, standing in the shadows
Smiling, amused at my feeble attempts
To draw you out into the daylight

I fish for you through an ocean
Of microfilm and microfiche
Not knowing if I've cast in the right direction
But I sense you lurking in the deep waters

Through graveyards I stumble
Looking for tombstone documentation
To find where you have ended
Your earthly sojourn
I want to exhume you from your paper trail coffin
And give you new life and a resurrected voice
To extract from you the secrets and essence
Of your existence

Seeking the relevance, the bridge
That connects US through common genes
The DNA strands that bind us together
As family

Perseverance by Alys Caviness-Gober

The Sycamore and the Ash by Jess Coovert

A tree sat in a meadow.
Alone and solitary. Its branches
Swaying in the warm summer
Wind that made the leaves sing.

One day the tree wasn't alone.

A girl came along and sat below.
Smoke was trapped in her irises,
Hair the color of fire, breathing
With the rays of the setting sun
And turning to liquid amber.
One day the girl wasn't alone.

The wind picked up, with it bringing
A cold winter that nipped at the
Bare leaves of the tree and much
Exposed girl. She curled against the
Wind, protecting herself like a flower.

One day the tree wasn't alone.

Branches now bare, with no
Leaves that once sang. Their
Voice taken by the harsh of
Winter's breath that took each
Lead, one by one.

Till all were gone and the girl,
She sat limp, wilted more like.
Slumped against herself as a frost
Took over. Her fiery hair now
Blackened and being pecked at
By the few animals brave enough
To go near such a creature.

Winter came and went. The
Grass now brittle and brown

By the summer heat, dead as the
Girl's hair that once glowed and
Swayed in the breeze with vitality.

The tree's leaves begin to fall,
Caressing the place where the rose
Once grew below it, like a lover
Would touch an empty bed where
A warm body used to lay.

One day, the tree wasn't alone.

The Sunset After A Storm by Sophie Doell

As a landscape photographer, I don't have full control over my
subject, and my plan to shoot a sunrise or sunset is often thwarted by
a storm. If the weatherman forecasts the rain to stop around sunset, I
go as planned and wait for the storm to stop.

I love watching the dark clouds slowly dissipate to reveal the golden
sunset. For a moment, the sky is painted with all hues of black, blue,
and gray, splashed with the golden colors of the sunset. My patience
to wait out the storm is then rewarded with the beautiful sunset photos
that have won prizes in photography competitions.

The experience is a reminder for me to remain hopeful during times
of hardship and sorrow in life. As I wait out the storm, the sky can be
so dark, it's easy to forget that a golden sunset can occur on a stormy
day just as on a sunny day.

Whenever I can't see the sunset through the clouds, that doesn't mean
the sunset no longer exists. In life, the darkness of sorrow or pain can
hide a joyous future like the dark clouds hide the beautiful sunset. But
in time, the dark sorrow and pain will dissipate as the bright golden
future becomes the present. Always hope and wait for that beautiful
sunset after a storm!

Morse Lake Sunset After A Storm by Sophie Doell

Our Favorite Recipe for Leftover Turkey[3] by Nancy Simmonds

Our son-in-law took this recipe home with him, served it to his school soupday potluck, and the next potluck day two other cooks brought the same dish. It's a winner!

Turkey Soup With Green Chilies

serves 6 (maybe . . . if you skimp)

Ingredients:

1 tablespoon olive oil
1 cup chopped yellow onion
1 clove garlic, minced
1 teaspoon chili powder
1 teaspoon salt
Freshly ground pepper to taste

---

[3] Recipe from *The Big Book of Soups and Stews* by Maryana Vollstedt copyright 2001, Chronicle Books

1 teaspoon cumin
1 teaspoon dried oregano
1 can (4 oz) diced green chilies, drained
4 cups stock or broth
1 can (14 oz) crushed tomatoes
2 cups cubed cooked turkey
2 cups corn kernels, fresh or frozen
¼ cup chopped cilantro or parsley

Toppings:

Grated Jack cheese
Broken tortilla chips

Preparation:

In a soup pot over medium heat, warm oil. Add onion and garlic and sauté until tender, about 5 minutes.

Add chili powder, salt, pepper, cumin, oregano, and chiles and mix well. This smells soooo good!

Add stock and tomatoes and bring to a boil. Reduce heat to medium-low and simmer, uncovered, about 10 minutes.

Add turkey, corn, and cilantro and simmer until heated through and flavors are blended, about 15 minutes longer.

Ladle into bowls and add toppings as desired.

Alys Purple Hair by Alys Caviness-Gober

(I like to write lyrics to my favorite songs. Here's my take on the great Roger Miller's classic, *Kansas City Star*.)

Got a email just this morning
It was sent from NYC
It was typed and neatly written
Offering me free studio space

And an agent to promote me
and sell all my abstract art
But I'm well-known here locally
I can't move; I'm a star

I go 'round my town
with my hair askew
and a-flying here and there
my flannels shirts
are paint-bespeckled
and my glasses match my hair

I'm the number one attraction
In the Walmart parking lot
I'm known as Alys Purple Hair
No thanks New York, thanks a lot

Alys Purple Haaaaaahhrrr
That's what I aaaaaare
Yoodle-oooh-delady you ought to see my car
I drive a big old minivan with duct-taped sides
and a panther on the hood
I got a table down at Copper Still
My life here's purty good

I'm the number one attraction
In the Walmart parking lot
I'm known as Alys Purple Hair
So no thanks New York, thanks a lot

Why I'm A Morning Person by Sarah E. Morin

My bed-fresh toes
are the first to leave prints
in the unbroken hours.

The most unpopulated
of the 24 timelands
is mine to explore.

This sand-eyed adventurer
lays claim
to uncharted day.

Sunset In The Valley by Leslie Ober

Into Position by Jenny Kalahar

You position each night for dreams,
white pillows a certain height for neck,
familiar blanket on or off
or fought over playfully
or roughly,
black darkness demanded
or hall light allowed to yellow under the door.
Silence as soundtrack
or spousal breathing
or rain pounding greyly on windows.
You position – a habit, a custom, a prayer
and wait on your back or stomach or side,
nude or pajamaed or gowned,
holding a hand
or letting your arms relax into their usual poses,
the dog's spine curved against your own.
You breathe in unison with the room's occupants
or lie alone, hearing the hairs in your ears violin
or lie alone, feeling no movement on the mattress
as no one rises a last time
after the bedroom light was doused.
Alone or accompanied, you wait,
slipping deeper
bracing
or longing for dreams
or enduring until they can be forgotten at dawn.
Smiling at the still-sleeping dog sharing your pillow
or at kind eyes just opening nearby
or frowning at nothing and no one,
you leave the warmth behind, adjusting blood flow,
cold feet hanging over an edge
remembering a wave of obligations
remembering what is real,
fading dreams detangling
through the colorless comb you inherited
or clouding the mirror as you brush your teeth.
Spitting away the last minty
or tasteless

or appalling remnants of the night,
you inhale wakefulness,
positioning for the day to come

"Zombies Can't Open Doors" by Michelle "Meesh" Payne

I am a coffee addict, a night owl, and a word nerd. Trust me, it has taken a lot of caffeine and many late nights to keep up my writing habit.

My love of words started as far back as I can remember. Around age 4, I decided to be an author when I grew up. In first grade, I wrote a play and it won a contest and kids actually performed it. The story focused on an elephant in a toy store, and I can't remember much else. Yet I do remember it was a milestone in my writing history.

Then middle school, high school, and college happened and with those years came countless essays, term papers, and creative writing assignments. I ended up as a Communications major with an English minor at a liberal arts college in a small town in Indiana. I went on to become a 25-year communications professional, and still going. One trick pony? Sometimes I think maybe . . .

But as the lifelong word nerd that I am, I have to say I'm quite proud when I see shades of the same within my two children, The Precious Pair. Nothing has stirred this pride in me more than a recent car conversation with my youngest.

This entire piece revolves around an analogy she created, but first let me comment on analogies. All good writers know their purpose is symbolic comparison, and they are to be used sparingly and creatively in one's writing. Nothing worse than an overdone analogy, otherwise known as a *cliché*. Word nerd writer types like to turn clichés on their heads with original spins.

My 10-year old's analogy was a true original, and ever since she mentioned it, I can't stop thinking about it:

HER: "Well, you know how zombies can't open doors?" (She asked me this matter-of-factly, as if everyone should know it already.)

ME: "No, I guess I never realized that, but it makes sense. Their arms aren't really functional, since they're dried up and dead, right?"

HER: "Right! So think about it, all of us are zombies when it comes to someone else's heart."

ME: "Okay, how do you mean?"

HER: "We are all zombies because we can't open the door to anyone's heart, unless it's our very own heartdoor to open. The zombies are my family and friends. They can lean and push against the door to my heart. But only I can decide to let them in."

ME: (Mind blown.) "Wow, I guess you're right. That's a pretty fantastic analogy."

HER: "Yes, and happy people let the zombies in. Unhappy people have a harder time letting them in, which is a little sad."

ME: "I agree. I'm glad that people like you and me let a lot of people, I mean, zombies into our hearts."

HER: "Me, too, Momma."
This recent exchange has led me to think deeply about the past year of my life and several different doors I've been leaning on and pushing on like a zombie. Personal relationships, career challenges, legal struggles, and real estate transactions, all included. The past 10 months have beaten me up on many days. But as in the analogy, a zombie doesn't feel pain.

Maybe that's why I keep pushing on some impossible-to-open doors so hard. I'm not allowing myself to feel the pain; that is, until one of the doorkeepers opens their door a tiny crack to say, *This one is not gonna' open for you, so why make a fool of yourself trying?*

Then reality sets in. I'm not a zombie after all. I'm a living, breathing, feeling, flawed, and – yes – sometimes foolish human being. And I've encountered my fair share of door slamming lately.

What do I mean? People whom I wish would heal who aren't ready to heal. Promotions I've gone for that I'm not going to get. Employees I want to hire with no budget to do so. The quiet cubicle I need that's still one year away in the blueprint. The price I ask for my house that no one is willing to pay. My moving date that keeps moving. A clear view of my future that appears only as a fogged mirror.

Wow, that's quite a list.
Yet, this list is *Life*.

Rejection.
Uncertainty.
Instability.
Disappointment.
Failure.

Sometimes we zombies need to take a step away from the locked doors to find different ones. Look for glass doors you can see into. Screened doors you can feel the morning breeze through. Colorful painted doors that welcome you. Automated doors with the silver button on the wall – even a zombie can lean against that button and open that door!

Find your doors. The ones that are meant and made just for you. The ones that joyfully fly open when they see you coming.

Matters of the heartdoors are complicated. That's why we have the expression "a change of heart." The muscle in our chest is not the most reliable tool for decision making. That's why I now insist on blending and balancing the emotions of what my heart tells me with the sensibility of what my brain tells me. The heart and brain work together to form the reliability of the gut instinct. The gut allows the door of the heart to stay closed for protective purposes, and in other cases to open more readily when the rewards just might outweigh the risks.

"There are no guarantees."
"Always listen to your gut."
"If it's not your door, it won't open."
What great clichés!

"Lean on your fellow zombies."
No cliché intended.

These deep thoughts were sponsored by my daughter, The Little Analogy Genius. I will encourage her to keep up with her word-nerding along with her number-nerding. (She's wayyyyyyy better at math than her sister and me.) In fact, I hope she keeps on nerding in general because we're going to need her and all the other young smart ones when the real zombies invade Noblesville.

Cometh, The Sun by Deborah Petersen

You, paean of color, of possibilities
You, marker of the next moment in this timelessness
Clarity, orange radiant
Understanding, pink rays
There will be births; there will be deaths this day
Grass and leaves will celebrate your life breath
Birds will harmonize your brilliance
That horizon, purple gray, silver light
Will become luminesce in promise
You come.
You come.
Again.

Nemesis by Dennis L. White

You stalked me since day one,
Lurking in the shadows,
Knowing I would never
Be able to get the upper hand.

In my youth I thought I was invincible,
I never heard your derisive chuckle,
You whispered my demise on the wind,
I would look over my shoulder
But never saw a thing
And would shake the chill away.

You hide in my subconscious
Mumbling, chanting your wretched mantra,
And as I get older your ghastly presence
Becomes more obvious and ominous
And my nightly slumber respite wanes.

Mountain Sunset by Leslie Ober

Not Taken from Proverbs by Jenny Kalahar

Bent so low she is nearly kneeling
she waits at the crossroad
under the light that changes from red to green to gold
rain not seeming to touch her
though it glints in every glow
of store and streetlight and phone
and she keeps dry the sidewalk beneath her shadow
never presses a button to cross
never expects a glance of care
and she is on the other side of heaven
and I am on the other side of heaven
watching through a café window
not rushing out
for I fear it would be the act
of a bird hurrying into a trap
a mouse rushing toward poisoned bread
and I would hear a snap
and fall and die and bleed and die and die
and so, I stay inside
where I may die a different way
and close my eyes
as I sip the blackness that may be hot coffee
listening to the whole world die, too

I Have No Illusions by Dennis L. White

~ Tribute to the latter writings of Rabindranath Tagore

I have no illusion
that whatever notoriety I have gained
will live on beyond my years here,

as the shore is wave swept in ceaseless motion,
my achievements will dissolve
and be reclaimed by the universe.
New generations will arise
and supplant the record of old,

anything of merit from my life
will be as a ripple in the pond
that fades until it is nonexistent.

What I carry away
is only what my heart holds
the love that was given away returns
the alms be multiplied,
the peaceful spirit endures,
nothing else matters.

The universe will not tolerate
hatred, violence or innocent bloodshed,
those atrocities die with the perpetrators.

I will be true to myself,
abhorring the abominable,
loving with full measure,
I leave not a legacy,
but a birthright . . .
honored.

My Sunrise by David Allen

You were my sunrise
after the dark days
of divorce, despondency,
and dead-end dreams.
Your smile delivered by phone
became a bright light,
guiding us toward
sunny island adventures
where America's day begins.
The start of a living fantasy
with my soulmate,
my Muse.

Untitled (haiku) by Chuck Kellum

I watch the sun set
Half a world away others
See it coming up

Day by Jenny Kalahar

Keep the body busy
and the brain
Bake cake and daily bread
Wash the soiled things of the household, of the self
Trim the lengthy
Grow the children upward
Fix the little damages as they come
Cling to what is needed, wanted
Toss seeds upon the soil and wait
while feeding everything and everyone who steps within
Take a book from off the shelf
Open pages and recite
Rake grass and gravel as it lies
Return unused fishing-worms to dirt
Paint the chipped and peeling once again in spring
Air the blankets
Mend the fences
Hang the wet things on the line
Stoke the fire, add more water to the kettle
Settle everyone to beds
Find a chair to sit in lamplight
Find a song to listen to
Recite a prayer you know by heart
And feel, oh feel this lengthy day
by fragments slipping away
And let it go with night's closing eyes
until another splashes in

Sky On Fire by Leslie Ober

Perspectives of a Solar Experience by Nancy Simmonds

Oh, when our golden sun sinks to the night
A rising sun does brighten other's day.
Here darkness gathers 'round and dims our sight
When golden sunbright sinks into the night

And leaves our way lit only by starlight.
Half 'round our sphere are greetings to dawn's rays
For when our golden sun sinks to the night
This sun does rise on someone else's day.

Garage Sale Blues by Steve VandeWater

Garage sale blues, I got garage sale blues
My wife just sold my bowlin' shoes
I got the damn garage sale blues

Well the yearly garage sale happened today
And I ain't got a lotta good things to say…
I got the mean old neighborhood garage sale blues
Oh, she sold my shit for pennies on the dollar
And when I found out you oughta heard me holler…
I got the cleanin' out the house again garage sale blues

Well, she sold my vinyl albums, even the doubles
If she sold 'em to a cop I'm prob'ly in trouble…
Got the 1970's marijuana smokin' blues
Double albums were the thing for separatin' your weed
And I reckon that a few of mine were still full of seeds…
Got the paranoid, home-grown, Indiana ditch weed blues

Garage sale blues, I got garage sale blues
Somebody bought my old game of Clue
I got the damn garage sale blues

Well our stuff cost over a thousand bucks
But we only made a hundred back and I think it sucks…
Got the buy high, sell low, bad investment blues
"This chair is marked a quarter. Will you take a dime?"
These people want to dicker with you every time…
Got the bargain hunter, low budget, redneck shopper blues.

Well a carload of kids I ain't ever seen
Come a' costume shoppin' for Halloween…
Got the retro wardrobe, outdated fashion blues

Well they stood in the driveway, lookin' and a laughin'
And it made me so mad, I wanted just to smack 'em…
Got the old guy, outta touch, cargo pants-wearin' blues

Garage sale blues, I got garage sale blues
I just can't win, I'm born to lose
I got the damn garage sale blues
If you've ever been there, you know it's true
You got the damn garage sale blues.

Evidence of Miracles by Jenny Kalahar

Wearing Crocs, she floats across puddles
feeling divine
the hydroplaning effect evidence
that she has touched the surface
but has not gone far below
though the other foot solidly touches ground each time
giving balance to the miracle

A cape of flannel pillowcase
taken from a clothesline
feels majestic on her shoulders.
She can fly
ten inches off the ground
as she hops from the edge of the sidewalk
back to reality too soon for joy

Her halo is a string of dandelion
some gone to fuzzy seed
adding to its pure resemblance
to the Holy Child's nimbus.
She can do no wrong while wearing it
and smiles an angelic smile
whisking it off a moment before
she tries to steal your heart

Carnations In Morning Light by Simona Buna

The Name Game by Bonita Cox Searle

I pressed my face against the chilled glass of the picture window in my grandparents' living room, watching the occasional car crunch along the road, tire chains pressing their patterns into the snow.

The snow covering our front yard was bright enough for sunglasses – not that anyone in my grandparents' house would own something so frivolous. No siree, Bob. Only young movie stars like Elizabeth Taylor or Audrey Hepburn wore sunglasses.

I longed to be out in that brightness, to stomp around, build a fort, maybe engage in a snowball fight or two. I wanted to run and laugh. I just had to spin around with my arms straight out from my sides through the cold snappy air.

No school today – no fourth-grade ups and downs. Grandpa was on dayshift, so the day promised to be a good one.

My grandmother's voice called me to come eat some breakfast.

I walked into the kitchen as slowly as I could. My mother sat at the dinette, her upper body rocking slowly back and forth, her eyes looking at nothing. She was a small woman with dreary brown hair caught in several places by little girl plastic barrettes.

My barrettes.

"Morning," I said as I pulled out a chair across from her. I knew that being as cheery as possible with grownups sometimes worked wonders.

I looked at her carefully as she rocked a little faster. She had been biting her lips again. I could tell by the thick scabs on her mouth. I poured some Twix into my Mickey Mouse Club bowl, wondering what I could do to get some kind of response from her.

"Silly rabbit! Twix are for kids!" I wiggled the cereal box up and down in front of her. No response.

"She's not feeling well," Grandma said as she moved around the table to the sink. According to her, either my mother wasn't feeling well or she was doing so much better. She said this mostly on the telephone or on the rare occasions she went to church with Grandpa and me.

"I'm fine." My mother sounded like a ghost. Her voice always seemed to come from a distant place that I couldn't see and would never find.

Her hands began to shake.

"Gerry," Grandma said. "Eat something. You need to build up your strength."

"No, thank you."

"Isn't the snow pretty?" I asked. "I sure would like to play out in that snow, wouldn't you?"

"Don't be silly," Grandma said. "It's too cold."

She turned on the hot water and poured a little Ivory liquid into the sink. I thought I heard a small sigh underneath the sound of the water, but I may have been mistaken.

I watched my mother for a few minutes more. Should I keep trying to get her attention? Sometimes I could make her laugh. Her laughter was like Tinker Bell and wind chimes all rolled into one. I lived to hear that laugh. If I pressed her too hard, though, she would wind up tight and start acting like a feral cat. No way to touch one of those.

I longed for her to be like the other moms in the neighborhood. Those mothers looked their children in the eye. They touched them, fed them, called them by name. I had a hard time remembering my mother saying my name, and I couldn't address her by any name at all without her becoming upset.

"Gerry," Grandma said again. "Eat something."

Again – "No." She got up from her chair and left the kitchen. I knew she was going to our shared bedroom. I just hoped she didn't lock the door this time.

I finished my breakfast and began my campaign to get out into that waiting snow. I knew Grandma didn't like me to do anything extreme and playing in zero degree weather counted as extreme. I begged and begged and begged until my grandmother threw her hands in the air and said, "Your nose will freeze up and break off if you go out there, but if that's what you want . . ."

She encased me in a couple of sweaters, a pair of corduroy pants, and a snow suit. She put gloves on my hands and mittens over the gloves. Then she rammed my double-socks covered feet into some snow boots. She put a bright cherry-red woolen hat on my head and wove a matching scarf around my neck. Both were birthday gifts from my father. He lived with my brother in the next state over. That hat and scarf set was my favorite present.

"There." she said. "You'll be back in five minutes, mark my words."

I was always having to mark Grandma's words since I had such a flighty nature. She scooted me out the door. The frigid air smacked against my cheeks. *Praise the Lord*, I thought as I squinted against the morning light.

No one else was outside.

If I stomped out a Fox and Geese pattern in the snow, surely someone would see me and come out to play. I ran around in a big circle several times to pack the snow down just right. Then I twirled in the middle of the circle to make a small round place where a "goose" could be "safe." Finally, I made the spokes from the center to the outer circle for the best game of tag in the whole wide world.

I looked around to see if anyone had taken the bait. Not a child in sight. No dogs or cats either. I ran around and around the circle to keep warm. I didn't want to go back into that house defeated. I wouldn't hear the end of it for the rest of the day. Grandma would call each of my aunts and tell them that I insisted on getting my own way again and how I was sure to come down with pneumonia and how hard it was to raise a child at her age and what an ungrateful girl I was, and then she would tell me the same thing.

I didn't need the reminder.

I heard a storm door bang and turned to plead with Grandma for just a few minutes more.

My mother hovered on the front stoop looking like Casper the Friendly Ghost. She wore a dingy white coat. No hat, no scarf, no mittens. How did she get away with *that*? My grandmother's face appeared briefly in the picture window, then disappeared.

"I want to play, too," my mother said.

"Sure!" I wanted to throw my arms around her and hug her hard, but I just ran up to her and tapped her on the back. "You're Fox!" I dashed onto the game path, so excited that I tripped over my own feet and smacked face first into the snow. I got back up as quickly as I could. I felt a thump on my shoulder.

My mother's laugh danced through the crisp, cold air. "One for me!" she said. My turn for Fox. I chased her up and down the spokes until I caught her around the waist.

"Please," I looked up at her. "Please, may I call you Mom?"

She pulled out of my grasp and bent over, gasping for air. "You may call me Gerry," she said. "All my friends call me Gerry," and she took off around the path again. She'd mixed up her turn, but I didn't care.

"Gerry," I called out just so I could say her name out loud. "Silly Goose! Look out for the Fox!"

I must have called her Gerry ten times that morning. "You're fun, Gerry." "Gotcha, Gerry." "Gerry" this and "Gerry" that until I was dizzy with joy and so full of hope that I could just burst with the fullness of it.

She dashed and weaved around that game path like she was a kid, her eyes bright with happiness. To me she looked like she had a reason to be on this earth, and I wondered at it. I wished that she would look that way when she saw me enter a room.

The screen door creaked again after what seemed like just a minute or two, and Grandma let us know hot cocoa and donuts were waiting inside, and that was a good thing, too. My nose was so frozen I thought it was going to shatter. Not that I would admit it.

I bounced through the door after Gerry and whispered to Grandma as I moved past her, "She said I could call her Gerry. She really did!"

"Well, now," Grandma said. That's what she usually said when she didn't want to commit herself. "Let's get you both warmed up and dry."

We slurped cocoa and munched donuts at the kitchen table like old chums, Gerry and me, as I chatted away about what we could do after lunch. Maybe play with my dolls or a game or two of Monopoly.

"Or," I tried to be nonchalant, "maybe you could read me a book."

I watched as the light in my mother's eyes dimmed like a cloud covered moon and her body began to rock.

"No thank you," she said.

I'd gone too far.

I went to her before she had time to get out of her chair. I wrapped my arms around her shoulders and kissed the top of her head. Her body stilled until I let her go.

"Never mind," I said to her retreating back, "perhaps another day."

Count to Ten by W.B. Cornwell

On days like these, I want to give up, just for a little while.
I want to lie on the cold, hard tile of the bathroom floor,
feel my skin lose its trapped in heat like fire in my veins.
Allow my tears to fall freely.
Take long and deep breaths
and count to ten.

Let the anxiousness melt away,
slowly stifling the list of worries and regrets that echo.
Bury myself in the isolation
and count to ten.

On days like these, I want to give up, just for a little while.
I remind myself to take long and deep breaths.
I tell myself to get up from the floor.
Count to ten
and smile and move on.

Discovering New Places by Leslie Ober

Sunrise In America by David Allen

I am waiting for sunrise in America
After this dark, broken night
Where democracy's been pummeled
By the clown chief's rubber mallet
And narcissistic scrawls on edicts
That devastate social programs
And reward the rich elite.

I am waiting for sunrise in America
To shine on the nation's capital
Where swamp creatures swim laps
Around the White House and Senate,
Where multitudes hurl protest chants
At their representatives' deaf ears,
And any change for the good is pending.

I am waiting for sunrise in America
The morning after votes are cast
To see if the clown prince falls
Or is enshrined as our new king
Bringing on the darker night and fog
Smothering what's left of our freedoms.

Sisters by More Than Blood by Nancy Simmonds

Three ladies giggle
heads close together
eyes sparkle
faces flushed as they leave the leather
of their saddle horses on the carousel.
One is sumptuous in Italian brocade
another in hiking boots and ruffled floral,
the third in American casual, cropped pants and braids.
Three Little Beauties in a July Forest Park
licking crumbs of Hummingbird Cake from their fingers
to the trilling tune of a meadowlark.
The taste of pineapple and banana lingers.

In October they walk arm in arm
costumed for the Medieval Faire
in slow perambulation of Cita's Italian home
pausing to taste rounds of corzetti and squash blossom there.
When fireworks light up the night
with happiness and peace in the air
the three good friends cheer the sight
of shared wonders extraordinaire.

June in Brazil with Nova as guide
hiking o'er mountains and into blessed caves
enthusiastic, wide-eyed
at the delicate art of wax flowers, saving
to heart their heavy scent
their velvet touch.
Their colors represent
the bloom and blush, the flashing eyes of three inasmuch
as can confirm
their faith in each other. Citadella, Nova Prata, and Noblesville
dancing, twirling, holding firmly
hearts clasped close in true good will.

I Love You, Little Wrinkly Butt by Leslie Ober

One of my children's favorite books is "I Love You, Stinky Face," by Lisa McCourt. So I have decided to write an adult version. The following is my parody.

One night, after crawling into bed, I began wondering what life would look like when we were older . . .

So I asked my dear husband . . .

"Hunny, what if I go gray in my 30s and it ages me by 15 years?"

And he answered, "I would play with your lovely, wiry hair and tell you, *I love you my wonderful, wise woman.*"

"But what if I gain a bunch of weight and have so many rolls that my belly button disappears?"

He said, "I would encourage you to continue eating healthy and tell you, *I love you my roly poly sweetie pie!*"

"But Hunny, but Hunny, what if the creases in my face grow so deep that food gets stuck in the folds?"

He smiled at me and said, "I would hold your lovely face in my wrinkled hands, help get the food out for you, and say, *I love you my sweet little chipmunk!*"

"Oh sweetie, but what if after having children my belly looks all stretched and striped like a tiger?"

"Then I would admire that beautiful belly that is proof of all of our wonderful blessings! And I would tell you, *I love you my tenacious tiger!*"

"But Hunny, what if my boobies sag all the way down to my belly button?"

He laughed at the imagery then said, "I would still hold them and enjoy them just as I did in our youth. And I would say, *I love you my saggy baggy babe!*"

"But Hunny, but Hunny, what if my eyes begin to fail me and I need big, thick glasses to help me see?"

"Then I will help you get around and offer to read to you every night. And I would tell you, *I love you my darling four eyes!*"

"Oh babe, but what if my wrinkled bootie begins to droop and looks like it's about to fall off my body?"

He chuckled and said, "I would still give you love taps as I walk by and tell you, *I love you my little wrinkly butt!*"

"But what if I lose all my teeth and have to wear dentures?"
"Then I will continue to adore your beautiful smile and tell you, *I love*

you my lovely, toothless wife! And if they needed to be cleaned, I will help you do that if you'd want me to!"

I stopped to think about all of these things and then wondered . . .

"But sweetheart, what if I lose my mind and can't remember anything or anyone anymore?"

"Then I will stay by your side always. I will love you well and do my best to remind you of all the wonderful memories we made together. I would never leave your side and make sure that we laugh often. I will speak life over you and remind you that we love because God first loved us. And I will tell you then as I tell you now: *I love you, my chosen bride. Outer beauty may fade as our bodies grow old, but the beauty that is in your heart will live forever! And I promise to love and cherish you until the day I die!*"

And with that, I smiled, hugged my hunny, and rolled over to go to sleep. Love is a beautiful thing!

The Gift by Vivianne Belle

Unexpectedly
it appeared

in splendor
there among the detritus

like a sunrise
on a Summer morning

moving with a softness
unhurried

sanding down
the dangerous edges

the sharp wreckage
of my life.

Sunrise on Mom's Angel, 23 June 2019 by Alys Caviness-Gober

Does She Know by Jenny Kalahar

Is she gone
does she know
are her shadows still connected
to her flowers as they grow

Are nasturtiums orange here
or are they yellow, are they dead
can we drink their milk like children
should we lace them on her head

Is she gone
does she know
if she's in heaven or on earth
will she take her shadow with her
or leave it for us to embrace

Are the willow leaves unwilling
to sway when she walks by

respecting that she has more grace
more devotion to the sky

Will the moon engorge and grow
into fullness if she wakes
at midnight should her dreaming path
bring her into consciousness again

Is she gone
does she know
has she left us
will she stay
will her shadow sit with us and guide us
mother creator, sister student, will she tell
other secrets she's not told us,
have we writ our poems well

Is she gone
does she know
has she left us
here behind
will she soar in loud procession
banging drums throughout the day
or will she bow to all her gardens' glories
and then sweetly slip away

Old Wives and Old Husbands by Jean Roberts

Old wives and old husbands
Old women and old men
Been together for a lifetime
Be together at the end

She's afraid to be without him
At the end of life alone
So even though it's ragged
That's why we go on & on

He always leaves the top off
So she always spills the juice
His nose & ears keep getting longer
But he hears and smells much worse

He's a glass of water
She's a glass of wine
Like a rosebush with the flowers gone
But the thorns still on the vine

Grumpy & frumpy arrive together
Here come toad & frog, rat & shrew
An old pine bench, an old wing chair
It's not fair how we see you

Old wives and old husbands
Old women and old men
Been together for a lifetime
Be together at the end

The Eclipse Of July 11, 1991[4] by Bonita Cox Searle

It lasted for six minutes and 11 seconds as
The moon moved from east to west
On that Indiana afternoon
Until it covered
Ninety percent of the sun.

Others watched through pinpricks in paper
Or peered through filtered telescopes,
But I sat on the concrete steps that sloped
Down my front yard
With my back to the eclipse
And watched the compressed illumination
Of the sun that remained
Divide the shadows of our beloved old maple tree
And its leaves,

---

[4] *Originally appeared on www.indianavoicejournal.com March 2017*

Our Chevy station wagon
With the faux wood panels,
Our Sears and Roebuck house,
Emma's hand-me-down bike,
Julia's scattered Barbies with the
Chopped off hair,
The remote control to David's battered toy robot,
Carmel the cat who lolled
On the warm sidewalk,
And me.

The shadows and their radiant outlines
Melted into the daylight
Too soon
As the moon progressed past the sun,
A part of the rhythm of the universe
That I wanted to savor for just
One minute more.

Sunrise by Chuck Kellum

The sun appears each morning.
That is nothing new.

But when that first glint
Of day splits the horizon,
Piercing the bubble of darkness
That has shrouded our dreams,
And bursts forth,
Shimmering with a hope
Which soon burns
Brightly
In all we do,

That dawning moment,

Is ever new.

Under a Dune by Steve VandeWater

We rented a cabin with a view of the sea
In the month of September, my sweetheart and me.
In pale autumn moonlight we'd stroll hand in hand,
The waves washing over the sand.

Well the season for tourists was long past its time
There was no one around us to witness my crime.
Now somewhere beneath the North Caroline' moon
My darlin' lies under a dune.

Oh, she loved the ocean, but was fearful to swim
she told me her brother had drown.
So I drugged her with liquor, then I drug her on in
And the cold water drug her on down.

Her fam'ly lay scattered, and her parents passed on
There were no close relations to notice her gone.
No good friends to wonder where my baby might be
And no one to blame it on me.

So I buried her body right under a sign
That protected the sandhills by posting a fine.
Now her grave marker serves to keep people away,
And keep the beachcombers at bay.

Oh, she loved the ocean, but was fearful to swim
she told me her brother had drown.
So I drugged her with liquor, and I drug her on in
And the cold water drug her on down.

Though her cries they fall deafly on other folks' ears
Still I've heard them nightly for twenty-odd years.
The wind through the sawgrass resembles her screams
Her spirit still haunting my dreams.

I once loved the ocean, now I'm fearful to swim
For both she and her brother have drown.
I'll nevermore enter into the salt sea

Lest their cold hands might drag me on down.
Oh their cold hands might drag me on down.
Yeah their cold hands might drag me on down.

I See Your True Colors by Leslie Ober

Cris' Chicken & Dumplings[5] by Alys Caviness-Gober

My husband Cris adapted this regular chicken and dumplings recipe to be dairy-free when our daughter had to give up dairy for several months due to her newborn's intolerance for cow's milk proteins.

That's not the same thing as lactose intolerance (which is a sugar issue), by the way. Approximately 2-3% of newborns experience Cow's milk protein intolerance (CMPI), which can cause them to have colic-like symptoms, and be wheezy, vomit, have diarrhea (including bloody diarrhea), constipation, a rash, eczema and/or a blocked nose. Most of them outgrow the intolerance by 1-3 years old. If anyone in your family has any trouble with milk proteins or sugars,

---

[5] Adapted from an Emeril Lagasse recipe for chicken and dumplings.

you can make this dairy-free recipe easy-peasy ~ and it actually tastes better than the dairy-filled version!

Ingredients:

2 split chicken breasts (on the bone with skin, about 3 lbs)
8 cups water
2 bay leaves
1-1/2 tsp salt
3 celery stalks, chopped
3 carrots, chopped
1 medium onion, chopped
1 tsp paprika
1/2 tsp dried thyme
1/2 tsp black pepper
1/4 tsp garlic powder
1 stick (1/2 cup) butter (dairy-free, use lard)
2/3 cup All-Purpose flour
1/4 cup cream (dairy-free, use coconut milk)
1/2 cup frozen peas

Preparation:

In a large pot or Dutch oven, add in split chicken breasts, water, salt and bay leaves.

Bring to a boil and cook over medium heat for 45 minutes. Don't boil too hard or too much water will evaporate. **Cris makes the following changes to this part:** cook the chicken in a pressure cooker with lots of additional celery, carrots & onions.

During that 45 minutes, you can chop your vegetables and make the dumplings.

Ingredients for the dumplings:

1-1/4 cups All-Purpose flour
2 tsp baking powder
1/2 tsp salt
2 Tbsp butter
1/2 cup milk (dairy-free, use coconut milk)

Preparation:

In a glass measuring cup, heat the milk and butter until butter is melted.

In a medium bowl, combine flour, baking powder and salt.

Add in milk and butter mixture and stir with a fork just until combined. Dough should be soft.

Turn out onto a floured surface and knead just a few times to make it come together (no more than 8 times).

Roll out to 1/8" thick and cut into 1" strips and then into 3-4" pieces. Cover with a damp towel until ready for them.

Meanwhile, after the chicken has cooked for 45 minutes, remove to a plate and let cool before shredding.

Remove bay leaves from the stock.

Add in the chopped vegetables and cook for 10 minutes.

In a separate small saucepan, melt butter and whisk in flour. Cook over medium heat for 30 seconds, stirring constantly to create a roux.

Gradually add in stock until thinned out a bit. Add roux mixture to the stock with the vegetables and whisk until no lumps remain.

Add in cream and peas. Bring to a light boil and add in the dumplings, one by one.

Stir gently, cover and cook for 10 minutes or until dumplings are tender and done.

Take off heat and add back in the shredded chicken. Stir to heat the chicken through and serve. Serves 4 - 6.

Enjoy!!

Leaving Something for the Future by Jenny Kalahar

Should I be accused of leaving something for the future
as if I contributed
as if I sat with pen or keyboard
twelve hours at a time
with the future in mind:
I did not.
It will come with or without me
with or without what I write
or leave behind as books of other writers
on my shelves
with or without the love I gave
the friendships attempted
the struggles to make my closer world better by an inch.
The future is less certain day by day
losing its humanity
children turning into statues breathing empty air

holding in their hands the answers to nothing
losing languages, creativity, individuality
forgetting faces, names and dates.
When the future is with you and yours without me in it
I'll be resting somewhere, watching
or hiding
willing the world to be strong enough
to remember its own history some day

Leaving Hell by Deborah Petersen

Recently, I left Hell.

I quietly slipped out the back door, out onto the sun-speckled
sidewalk, and felt breath, a breath so deep and so unfamiliar that my
lungs nearly burned with joy. What was that nightmare? Where was I
that my Soul ached minute by minute, my capacity of Compassion
drained into the vortex, my silent screaming to *Wake Up*, to cry no
more tears? There was so much healing to be done, so many
connections to be made, such much pain to be lessened, but, not there,
not in the Hell. Those who live there and thrive are brutal to others,
self-absorbed, dictatorial, condescending, lacking all wisdom of
connecting with others, cannot feel and can only fill out the forms.
There is no place for care and concern in their ego lives, their first-
person singular pronoun existence. All relationships are problems,
self-created. Staff meetings were temper tantrums and sharings of
slighted visions. There was no support, no dignity, no full picture
perspective, no place in the universe, only in their own verbs.

I died there, daily.

Where can I touch to heal you? Where can I meet you to help
alleviate your pain? What shall we explore together for your Journey
is mine as well? These were always my first questions. Yet, there was
no time and no place and no box to complete in this Hell for these to
be asked.

You see, not too long ago, I had the chance to slip away to Santa Fe,
into that same sun-speckled sunshine, to be immersed in another

world, another much more beautiful garden. The people there knew and lived Compassion and Love, their Narratives taught so much in their Basho lives and tasks completed. This was authentic. This was so true and the possibilities made me dizzy.

My faith on so many levels was renewed; my tears were not of pain but of luminescence, a brilliance that strobed the universe and gave light to the stars. I fell on my knees, deeply, and bowing to that within me, how I was touched, and shaking in the epiphany of the moment. This was the gift that the spiritual retreat in Sante Fe was meant to give me all along. This was the slight nudging at dawn for me to awaken and to scream, ***Thank You! I am ready to Serve!***

I sit here, breathing. Breathing deeply, contentedly, happy. I now know Hell. I know its taste, its stench, its cacophony. I know its falseness, its pain, its false power. I will forever be grateful that I was able to find the strength to climb out, to wash off the indignities and cesspool existence, and to feel the sun, to breathe, and to know that I have within me the grace of Service, my God-Given Gift, my Divine Love.

Morning Song by Dennis L. White

In the pre-dawn hours of the new day
Birds sing in chorus their morning anthem
Pleading, beseeching, eye of the sky to open
To cast golden rays upon the night weary world

They sing with the fervent zeal of expectation
Knowing that it is their song that entices
The waking orb to rise from its bed of slumber
To sparkle nocturnally deposited dew drops

Morning song is not a burden but a joy
Their varied voices and trills fly to the heavens
Praising the Giver of light and day
In acknowledgment and thanksgiving

Morning Song by Simona Buna

Rising by Jenny Kalahar

A sparrow waits, hopping
impatient for a magic carpet made of crumbs
reminding me of something I feel but can't write

A distant howl of dog or lonely heart
smokes out of the alley over the cowfield
reminding me of something I feel but can't speak

A light goes out that I was using to read your letter
leaving me at the beginning of the last paragraph
reminding me of something I feel but can't see
A door swings without being moved

by hand or by air or by yearning
reminding me of something left open
or something closed and never thought of again

Our sun rises over harvested, splintered cornstalk debris
without a visible entity beneath, pushing
reminding me of resilience that comes after a dark time
and I breathe it in, turning golden as I, too, float and rise

I Didn't Get Up Yesterday by Tim A. Baker

I didn't get up yesterday
Can't make this feeling go away
It seems the world is upside down
And there is bad news all around
I don't know quite what to say
I didn't get up yesterday

Don't even know what I could do
Not sure that 1 and 1 is 2
All the facts aren't adding up
But I'm sure I've had enough
Nothing's changing day to day
I didn't get up yesterday

I want to scream, and I want to shout, yeah, yeah
But I fear, there's no way out . . .

Let's hope for better days ahead
If they don't come I hope I'm dead
Cause I just can't stay the course
It looks like things are getting worse
And so I won't get up today
It doesn't matter anyway

I want to scream, and I want to shout, yeah, yeah
But I fear, there's no way out . . .

Moonlight and Morning by W.B. Cornwell

What is the morning dew?
It is tears shed from the fading night
The night weeps as it says farewell

Before the sun rises bringing day anew
When the earth is still covered in the moon's light
and the world is a living Gothic fairytale

A purple velvet sky stretches above
Listen to the owls and crickets as they join in song
And nocturnal beasts and winged creatures have their say

The moon looks soft to the touch like a silken glove
But as always, night will end before too long
and so the evening will weep at the break of day

Aw, the morning finally does shine
Bringing the golden sun and choruses of birds
Feeling warmth as rays meet your face

All seems so perfect, so simply divine
It is almost hard to find the words
As I sit her and take in the beauty of this place

The Yard Sale by John Gilmore

I grabbed a for sale sign
to stick in my yard
I'm not much of a salesman
but it can't be that hard
to clean out my closets
and from under the bed
If I no longer use it
I should sell it instead
'cause I'm about out of room
I need a little more space
Got a lifetime of stuff

all over this place
Maybe some to Goodwill
and some to the trash
but there might be a few treasures
that could bring me some cash

So, I'm having a yard sale
with bargains galore
on all sorts of things
I don't need anymore
Just need 'em gone
Out of sight out of mind
So pull in my driveway
and see what you might find

Got several of these
and too many of those
Some barely used tools
and bags of old clothes
I spread out the clothes
on the living room floor
saw an old favorite T shirt
faded and worn.
Then a box of old photos
I just can't throw away
Sentimental reminders
of my younger days
Grabbed the next box
and opened the lid
Souvenirs I'd held onto
since I was a kid

So, I'm having a yard sale
with bargains galore
on all sorts of things
I don't need anymore
Just need 'em gone
Out of sight out of mind
So pull in my driveway
and see what you might find

With piles to the left of me
and piles to the right,
I could be stuck here sorting
through this shit all night
Who knew this job
could be so damned hard?
I just pulled that for sale sign
back out of my yard

> *Now there'll be no yard sale*
> *with bargains galore*
> *I'm keepin' all of this stuff*
> *and I'll probably get more*
> *So it's back in the closets*
> *and under the bed*
> *That yard sale can wait*
> *'til after I'm dead.*

I used to ride my bike to Noblesville where the pretty girls lived.
by John Stewart

I first noticed them in eighth grade. These were the days when all the high school basketball teams in the county would face off in the Sectional Tournament. Pretty much everyone in the county had a ticket or listened over the radio. I went with my two best friends. As 8th graders, we wouldn't really watch the games but would just walk around the top of Carmel's gymnasium talking to other non-high schoolers. It was there that I first spotted them. Something about tight blue jeans, big hair, and rabbit fur jackets sparked my interest. They were so much more exotic than the girls that lived south of 146th street. It's hard to believe it now, but there used to be country roads between Carmel and Noblesville and after our new discovery, these roads would be well traveled by my ten-speed.

There was Mary, the cheerleader that every boy wanted, and her friend MeMe, who had the better personality. MeMe was the one a wise man would pick as his girl, but none of us was that wise in junior high. And then there was Meg, the confident, self-assured girl that was smarter than any boy in Hamilton County. And she still is today.

A few years later, after I had ditched the bike for my first car, I still traveled those country roads and I met the most beautiful girl that lived in Noblesville. It wasn't the long hair, pretty face or perfect smile that made Amy beautiful. It was the fact that Amy truly personified LOVE. She was even born on Valentine's Day. Everyone that knew Amy, loved Amy. She found value in everyone and everything around her. Amy made you feel special and when you are an awkward teenage boy, Amy was the flame you flew towards in the dark. Every time you were around Amy, she embraced you with love and sparked something inside of you.

I grew up in newer suburban neighborhoods and my parents found significance in a large home and social acceptance. Carmel was perfect for them. They both came from nothing and worked hard to provide for their family. I was fortunate to have parents that provided well for us and loved each other. Unlike me, Amy lived in a historic home just off the Noblesville Courthouse Square, and she had something that was new to me . . . Amy had a single mom.

Her mom was artistic and full of energy. She had a loft bed in her bedroom, an art studio above their garage and seemed completely happy being a single mom, artist, and human. She demonstrated that you didn't have to conform to societal norms or have a big home, big job or big car to be happy. She just was. It really shouldn't have surprised me that Amy was raised in this type of household, with a mother who celebrated life and love.

It's been 40 years since that sectional tournament. I moved away for college and stayed away for over 20 years living in California, Texas, Tennessee, and Oregon. But when I decided to return to Indiana, those ladies and that old house on Hannibal Street had impacted my life. I wanted to live in a small century home with wood floors and comfy furniture rather than in a newer neighborhood. I wanted to walk and shop around the Courthouse Square instead of a strip mall. I wanted some of the peace, joy, and love that I experienced at Amy's house. I wanted to take my own pretty girl to Noblesville and make it our home. So, I did.

And now my son has found his own pretty girl from Noblesville.

Sunrise by Tim A. Baker

A Heart on Fire by W.B. Cornwell

The ballroom in the Gallagher's New Port home was full of the delightful scent of jasmine that evening in 1936. The mirrored walls, framed with gilded robes and tassels, reflected the guests, the best families on the coast. Men in tailored tuxedoes and women in fine dresses of silk and lace adorned with precious jewels that shimmered in the light.

Beatrice Virginia Gallagher was a living dream. Her hair was golden blonde, her blue eyes were alight, and her lips were full. Her figure was the envy of all other girls in her social circle. All of the young men – eligible or not – often remarked on her beauty. She was of good breeding and as elegant as any girl could hope; shy and sheltered, yet on the edge of something absolutely scandalous. The only jewels she wore that night were small pearl earnings and a silver ivy hair comb. She was a vision in her pink dress as she glided down the stairs and into the foyer where her parents stood. Her father was a tall and plump man with a kind face partly hidden by his thick black mustache. Her petite mother glared at her, disappoint plain in her stern eyes.

"Princess, you look lovely," her father said with a kiss on her cheek.

"You should have worn the dark blue dress," her mother chimed in. "John Glaser likes blue."

"Why should I care what color John Glaser likes?"

"Because John Glaser is from the best family in the state, and as you are well aware, he is interested in making you his wife."

The band started to play a song. "I'm going to dance," she said with a sigh.

"Beatr – " Her mother started after her until her husband took her by the arm and gave her a warning look.

"Let her have some fun. After all, you only turn eighteen once."

As Beatrice walked into the room, all heads turned to her, and those on the dance floor stopped to applaud her. Her cheeks flashed red as cherries. As she greeted her guests, a hand tapped her on the shoulder, and she turned to see a young man with a muscular build, slicked-back dark brown hair, and deep green eyes. It was John Glaser, the man Beatrice's mother picked for her long ago. In his hand was a green velvet box. She swallowed hard, worried about what might be in the small box.

"I hope you don't mind opening my gift first," he said with a smile. "I know it isn't time yet, so this may seem a bit unorthodox, but I can't wait to see you open it."

As he handed her the box, she could feel her heart about to jump from her chest. Beatrice liked John Glaser, but she didn't see herself with him. Yes, he was handsome. Her friends thought she was lucky to be his pick. He was also polite and from a good family, and money would never be a worry with the heir to the Glaser fortune as a husband. But still, John never made Beatrice feel like her heart was on fire – this could not be a great romance like in the books she read. She slowly opened the box and saw a cluster of diamonds in the shape of a heart. To her relief, it was just a broach.

"Thank you, John," she said as she closed the box.

"Darling," her mother's voice called out from behind her. "Let me help you with that. John wouldn't have given it to you had he wanted it to stay in the box." She laughed.

"Very true, Mrs. Gallagher." He smiled. "And might I add you look lovely tonight – almost as lovely as your daughter. One might mistake you for sisters."

"John Glaser, you flatter me," she said as she pinned the broach to Beatrice's pink dress.

The bandleader waved his wand and the band started to play another song. John asked Beatrice to dance. She agreed to out of social obligation. As they took the floor, spinning and gliding to the jazzy tune, he looked into her eyes. "I hope you are having a good birthday."

"I am."

"Before the night is over, I have a question I must ask you. But I want you to enjoy your party for a little longer," he said as he held her tighter.

"Alright," she said. She tried to pull away, just an inch or two. When the dance ended, the band started to play the birthday song and the guests all sang. A cart with a large, white, four-tier cake with pink roses was wheeled to her with eighteen candles lit on top. She struggled to reach high enough to blow them all out, but she managed. The guests clapped and she looked around to see John shaking her father's hand as her mother smiled. She knew what that meant. John Glaser would ask her to marry him with the blessing of her parents, and she would have no option but to say yes. She could feel the room spinning; she was now and forever trapped. She smiled at a few of her guests as she moved towards the door.

Her mother cut her off and grabbed her by the shoulders. "Where do you think you are going?" she said angrily through a forced smile because people were still near. "Thank you for coming," she told two of her society friends, who smiled in return.

Beatrice said, "I need some air."

"Do not make a spectacle of yourself. This is your party – you can't just leave."

"My party!?" she shouted.

"Shh." Her mother stared daggers at her. "Mind yourself."

"No, Mother. This party is for you. For you to show off for your friends." It was the first time Beatrice Gallagher had ever told her mother how she felt, and after eighteen years of built-up emotions, it felt good.

"How dare you?" she whispered harshly. "Everything I've done, I've done for you. You've been to the best schools, you've only worn the best clothes, you have more fine jewelry than any other girl in this city. Summers in Paris. Winters in Aspen. Now, I have given you John Glaser. Everything is set. You will never need to worry with him."

"Mother, I don't – "

"I don't care," she interrupted. "Marrying for love is not the most important thing in the world. You will learn to love him." She ran her hand across the front of her hairline, fixing a few loose strands. "Before the clock strikes ten o'clock, John will ask you to marry him and you will agree."

"As I said, I need air."

"Be back in half an hour."

Beatrice walked out of the ballroom and through the foyer. Her heels clicked on the tile as she picked up speed darting down the long hall and into the dining room, making her way into the kitchen. There she saw him. He was leaning against the table, biting into a red apple, the juice trailing down the corner of his mouth.

"Excuse me, miss." He wiped the sweet and sticky juice from his face.

"Who are you?" she asked, looking him over. He was tall and thin with unruly black, curly hair. His attire was shocking to her. He wore dark gray slacks, a white shirt was white, and a black vest left unbuttoned. She had never seen a grown man without a jacket and tie inside her home. He was like an unkempt he-man that Gable would have played. For the first time in her life, Beatrice could feel that heat – a flaming heart was pounding inside her chest. This was the feeling she had been waiting years for. This is the feeling that John Glaser could never give her.

"I'm Darren Price," he said with an awkward smile. "I'm with Allen and VanBuskirk. We provided the booze for this shindig."

"Oh." She looked puzzled still.

"About an hour ago we got a call to bring some reinforcements. You high society folks drink a lot," he laughed.

"Why are you still in my kitchen?"

"Since the order was short notice, a lady let me in – the cook, I guess – and she gave me a plate of food and this apple as a tip."

"Ah, that sounds like Maggie." She smiled. She felt so out of sorts looking at him, not knowing what to say or what to do.

"I can finish this on the road." He turned and headed toward the door.

"Wait."

He spun around.

"Don't go. Please, I don't mean to be rude. Stay and finish your food."

"Are you sure you don't mind?" he asked.

"Of course not." She walked closer to him, leaning against the table as if inviting him back to his original position.

"What is this big party for, anyways?" He took another bite.

"My birthday," she said quietly. She looked down at her high heels.

"Happy birthday, miss!"

"Thank you. Please, call me Beatrice."

"Beatrice," he said with a smile.

She could feel herself blushing. There was something powerful about hearing his raspy voice say her name.

"Beatrice," he said, making her heart skip a beat, "I hope you are having a good birthday so far." He sat on the edge of the table.

She looked to him, smiled, and hopped up onto the table herself.

"Honestly, nothing about it has been too great."

She couldn't believe that she was talking to a total stranger, let alone a man who worked for a liquor shop. Countless generations of women in her family must have been rolling over in their graves.

"It is just another birthday party so my mother could invite people over to show off the house. I heard her mention to at least five people the new chandelier we had imported from London. Everything is about appearance."

He looked at her, their eyes meeting, feeling her desire to be free. Never did he think someone who possessed everything could have utterly nothing in their life. He placed his hand on her knee and he felt her tremble. He looked her up and down before staring at her lips. He got down from the table and looked into her eyes for a long moment. He took her flawless face in his hands, then kissed her. She wrapped her arms around him pulling him close to her. He moved his lips from hers to her cheek and trailed down to her neck and shoulder and back up again. She let the fire in her heart consume her. He stopped kissing her, looked into her eyes again, but kept his body pressed to hers.

"Tell me, Beatrice, what do you want for your birthday?"

"I want to run. I want to get out of this house and see what trouble we can get into before sunrise," she said before kissing him again.

December Sunrise, Noblesville by Lori Cates Hand

The world is heavy on my shoulders these days.

My father has recently been moved to memory care and it's a difficult, if not unthinkable, adjustment. I'm losing faith in the goodness of human nature and am watching everything and everyone

I always took for granted slipping away. It's a wonder to me how I manage to keep going. But I do.

The morning after my birthday, I rose before dawn, showered, dressed, and went downstairs to the kitchen to wait for my daughter to be ready for me to drive her to the high school on my way to work. As usual, I was making the most of waiting by unloading and loading the dishwasher and starting a load of laundry. Suddenly I was arrested by the moment of sunrise outside my kitchen window. The stunning palette jolted me out of my routine.

I shrugged into my down jacket, slipped on my shoes, and hurried out to the frosty backyard to catch this shot on my phone. Taking time to be present in that moment recharged me enough to take on another day.

Sunrise by Lori Cates Hand

International Connection Section

Sponsored by Love's Hangover Creations

Seeking Refuge In The Sun by Ndaba Sibanda

Messages come in many shapes, sizes, and colors, but what is crucial is how we interpret and implement them.

If friendships, relationships, or marriages were scripted like plays and movies, life would not be as dramatic and enigmatic as we know it to be. We write and practice our scripts as we live, love, and transition.

I love the sky. How magic it is to marvel at that celestial dome as it towers above the Earth. I begin to visualize daylight and the delight of sightseeing birds and insects as they fly in their sky; I bask in the cordiality and cuddle of the sun, and wander away in a trance into the wonder of the clouds, lightning, and rainbows before arriving at the constellations; I then go clubbing with the night and its stars, and the moon (though the stars hog the limelight!); finally I decide to hang out with precious Precipitation's dear family and friends, I mean lovely and lively chaps like Rain, Hail, Drizzle, Sleet, and Snow.

What fun! No company beats their watery warmth, harmonies, and hospitality, I swear!!

I love the wilderness in the form of wild animals, forests, vegetation, rocks, rivers, and beaches. These amazingly beautiful things go about their business despite human intervention. Bravo!

People, the preservation of the universe – which is the natural, physical, or material world – is essentially the preservation of life, and this cause is close to my heart.

Baba's Stuffed Peppers by Alys Caviness-Gober

You can stuff a pepper with just about anything, I know, but this recipe is my favorite. I learned it from my Baba (my mom's mom), who immigrated from Macedonia to the United States in 1940 (with my three-year-old aunt and my one-year-old mother). I cook like my Baba did: no measuring, just a "throw it in a pot" style. So, you can adapt the amounts of meat, currants, pine nuts, and spices to suit your tastes.

It's a pretty simple recipe, it's both pretty and yummy, and, in case you make too much stuffing (like I always do!), you can eat the leftover stuffing as a side dish all by itself. Cold or warmed, it's really good!

Ingredients:

Yellow, red, orange, and green peppers ~ I use at least 8 whole peppers, two of each color.
Rice ~ I prefer Basmati white rice; I usually cook up about 4 cups of rice. Follow rice package instructions for cooking your rice.
Grapeseed Oil (you can use your choice of oil, but I use grapeseed oil because it doesn't change the flavor of the food (unlike olive oil).
About 2 lbs lean ground beef (you can also use a half-n-half beef-lamb mix).
1 finely chopped onion (yellow or white; your choice)
1 box of dried currants
1 pack of pine nuts (optional if there are nut allergies to worry about)
To taste: salt (don't be shy with the salt when cooking the meat!), black pepper, paprika, basil (dried or fresh), a tad of oregano (dried), a tad of sage (dried)

Preparation:

Pre-heat oven 350°-375°.

Wash and cut off the tops of the peppers; keep the pepper-lids if you want to put them on top of your stuffed peppers whilst they cook (that's optional). Clean out all the seeds and membranes from the insides of the peppers.

Spray or wipe a roasting pan with your choice of oil.

Cook your rice in appropriate-sized saucepan. I cook mine to an *al dente* state, because the rice will absorb more moisture and oil (from the meat) when inside the peppers.

Cook your onion and meat in appropriate-sized skillet ~ I use grapeseed oil and first cook down the onion (until browning and translucent). Add some of the salt, black pepper, paprika, and the other herbs to the onion, and then add more of those ingredients to the meat. I poke at the meat whilst it cooks, breaking up any lumps because I don't like lumpy ground meat! Browned edges are yummy, BUT be sure you cook the meat thoroughly!

In a large bowl, mix up your rice and meat, adding the currants and pine nuts. Taste it to make sure you have the right amount of salt, spices, herbs, *etc*. Add more if needed.

With a spoon, stuff your peppers ~ I usually end up using my hands, especially to press down the stuffing into each pepper (I like 'em well-stuffed!), so you might want to have a fresh unused pair of kitchen prep gloves handy.

Place a rack in your baking/roasting dish, add water to just touch the bottom of the rack.

Place your stuffed peppers upon the rack; place the pepper-lids on them if you want (optional). The peppers can fit tightly in the pan. Depending on the size of your pan, and how many peppers you're making, you may need two pans.

Cover with aluminum foil and cook in pre-heated oven at about 350-375° until peppers are softened to the point you desire. Again, I like *al dente* stuffed peppers; some people like 'em really mushy. Your choice.

Optional: you can remove the aluminum foil for the last 10 minutes or so of cooking, if you want.

The peppers can cook as you cook other dishes, by the way ~ basically you are just warming up the stuffing and cooking the peppers to your desires softness.

Serve on a pretty platter, or right out of the pan. Enjoy!

Her Sunshine by Ndaba Sibanda

That was none other her one and only son,
Of him she would say: *he's a ray of sunshine
In my life. He's my source of glee and pride.*

Dream Fractal by John Caviness

What The Dawn Of A New Day Means by Ndaba Sibanda

A new day gives birth to efforts and expectations
A new day heralds an opportunity for experiences

A new day is a providential bonus and blessing
A new day could mean a promising turning point

A new day beckons to be greeted with power
And positivity if not with hope and happiness

A new day may present new horizons and heights
And foundations for renewal, rebranding, or rearming

A new day is reason enough to celebrate a heart's palpation
A new day sets a platform for the mind and soul to jell together

Schlaf ein (Fall Asleep) by John Caviness

Schlaf ein Original Artist: Lindemann
© Writer(s): Peter Taegtgren, Till Lindemann
German lyrics, Album Version, from
https://rammwiki.net/wiki/Schlaf_ein_(song)#Lyrics
English lyrics interpretation by John Caviness

Although I haven't seen the 2018 musical, *Hänsel und Gretel*, from where this song originates, I can imagine how well it fits into the show. Songwriters Till Lindemann (of German bands *Rammstein* and *Lindemann*) and Peter Tägtgren (also of *Lindemann*) became involved in the theatrical production because Till's daughter was involved in it. In this lullaby-*esque* song, the initially calming but eventually rousing piano notes mix with Till's deep vocals, creating a soundscape of uncertainty for the listener, one that you don't need to know German to feel deeply.

The song prompts the listener to consider several questions. First, there is uncertainty surrounding who is singing to whom. Is the forest a figurative representation of a dreamland? Or is it the forest in the fairy tale, that the two children find themselves lost in? Could this be a sinister lullaby from a fiend in the forest, or an inspiring memory of a parents' song?

The Grimm fairy tales with which we are familiar aren't very pleasant; the original texts can be quite sinister. Till's somewhat sharpened vocal delivery of otherwise pleasant lyrics opens up a darker interpretation than you might expect. The raised key change towards the end of a song, a musical tool also known as modulation, emphasizes previously repeated lyrics in this song, thus adding to emotional interpretation of the lyrics themselves.

What drives this song home for me, as a German speaker, can be found in the last verse and chorus. The language used, from a parent's perspective, paired with the notable key change near the end of the song, begets a sense of sorrow and joy, wrapped in package that hits close to home to both parents and children. *Und so Gott will, sehen wir uns wieder*, rings like a prayer of a parent who long hasn't seen his or her children.

A number of the songs from the play can be found on the *F&M* Album, which was released on 22 November 2019 and can be found where most music for purchase is available.

Schlaf ein

Wenn ihr Kinder müde seid
Spricht euch Gevatter Schlaf Bescheid
Er steigt vom Schattendach der Bäume
Holt euch in sein Reich der Träume

Wenn ihr euch matt und schläfrig fühlt
Hat er sanft euch schon umhüllt
Nun ist es Zeit nichts mehr zu tun
Geist und Körper auszuruhen
Im tiefen Wald, man sieht nichts mehr
Wird es euch ums Herz so schwer

Wenn der Tag zu Ende geht
Das letzte Licht vor Dunkel steht
Du sollst nicht traurig sein
Morgen wird die Sonne scheinen
Schlaf ein

Ach, die kleinen Herzen schwer
Und die Tränen fließen sehr
Da ist doch gar kein Blut zu sehen
Ihr müsst jetzt schlafen gehen

Liebes Kind, du sollst nicht weinen
Davon wird nur die Erde nass
Morgen wird die Sonne scheinen
Leckt dir die Tränen von den Wangen blass

Wenn der Tag zu Ende geht
Das letzte Licht vor Dunkel steht
Du sollst nicht traurig sein
Morgen wird die Sonne scheinen
Schlaf ein

Und ist die kalte Nacht vorbei
Gibt der Schlaf euch wieder frei
Öffnet sanft die schweren Lider
Und so Gott will, sehen wir uns wieder

Wenn der Tag zu Ende geht
Das letzte Licht vor Dunkel steht
Du sollst nicht traurig sein
Morgen wird die Sonne scheinen
Schlaf ein

Fall Asleep (interpretation by John Caviness)

If you children are tired,
Let Godfather Sleep know.
He'll climb from the shadowy treetops,
To bring you to his kingdom of dreams.

If you feel weak and drowsy,
He'll hold you gently and embrace you.
Now it is time to do nothing more,
But rest your mind and body.
In the deep forest, one sees nothing,
This will make your heart so heavy.

When the day comes to an end,
The last light stands before darkness.
You shouldn't be sad.
The sun will shine tomorrow.
Fall asleep.

Now little hearts grow heavy,
And the tears flow steady.
There is however, no blood in sight,
You must now go to sleep.

Sweet child, you shouldn't cry,
This only turns the Earth wet.
The sun will shine tomorrow,
Just lick the tears from your cheeks.

When the day comes to an end,
The last light stands before darkness.
You shouldn't be sad.
The Sun will shine tomorrow.
Fall asleep.

And then the cold night has passed,
Sleep sets you free once again.
Gently open your heavy eyelids,
And God willing, we will see each other again.

When the day comes to an end,
The last light stands before darkness.
You shouldn't be sad.
The Sun will shine tomorrow,
Fall asleep.

Son Rise by Leslie Ober

Love Died by Leslie Ober

Bleeding, beaten
But never broken
Sweating, pleading
But there was no other way
Whipped and wounded
But never weakened
Perfection pierced
Tortured, hanging in agony
Paying the price
The Prince of Peace
In pain, suffering
The weight of the world
On His shoulders
And then He breathed His last breath
"It is finished."
Heaven gasped
The veil was torn
The Creator died
For His creation
The King gave up everything
The ultimate sacrifice
The sinless Teacher
Became the sin of man
Love came
He served, He healed
He taught, He lived
He led, and then
Love died.

But Love is Alive by Leslie Ober

He didn't just die
The Lover of my soul
was crucified
He hung in agony
Carrying the weight
of every burden,
of every man.

Fear, hatred,
anger, confusion
settled in.
How could this have happened
to our King?
For three days,
silence, heartache
replaying memories,
recounting stories
from this Son of God,
this Son of man.
The darkness hovered.
Tears stained pillows.
Broken hearts cried out.
What now?
WHY?!?
But in an instant
everything changed;
from utter sorrow
to abounding joy,
from wounds
to scars
from death
to LIFE!
His tomb is empty!
Doth our eyes deceive us?
No! He has beaten death!
Our Jesus is ALIVE.
Nail-pierced hands
offer proof for the doubting;
His words strangely familiar.
He has not left us after all!
Love died.
But now,
Love is ALIVE!
In you,
In me.
Forever He will be.
Alive, alive.
The Risen King!

A Dance With Nature And Life by Ndaba Sibanda

They thirsted for a touch of freshness
A touch to wash away their dryness

A new week ushered in: Sunday morning greeted them in style
A pleased pair of ears received pattering sounds: a dream shower

It poured down and enriched the land. Nature's love was live!
Land was quenched of thirst, plants healed of pangs of dehydration

Rivers roared in celebration, dams hugged inflows in humming ways
Farmers were ready to farm, fauna and flora flourished as if feted

Percy Fawcett Cocktail by Alys Caviness-Gober

I invented this drink whilst watching *The Lost City of Z*, which is
about British explorer Percy Fawcett, who mapped and explored
significant areas of the Amazon River. The drink is both pretty and

yummy! It's a good holiday drink because it's made with fresh cranberries and it looks so pretty with a green lime wedge garnish, but you can enjoy it any time (I do!).

Cocktail Ingredients:

Ice cubes
Cranberry-Lime Simple Syrup
Ginger Ale
2-4 Limes: slices (for simple syrup) and wedges (for garnish)
Alcohol of your choice (whiskey, silver tequila)

Ingredients for Cranberry-Lime Simple Syrup:

Water
Sugar
Cranberries (fresh)
Limes sliced
Optional: Herbs and Spices of your choice

Make a Cranberry-Lime Simple Syrup:

FYI: Simple Syrup is made with equal parts water and sugar, so you get to decide how much you want to make!

In a sturdy saucepan, bring to boil your water, sugar (I used a couple cups each), fresh cranberries (I used one full bag), lime slices (I used two limes), and any herbs and spices you want to add. Fresh herbs are best, but I didn't have any the first time I made this, so I used dried sage, basil, and coriander, but you can use your favorite herbs/spices.

Turn burner down to bubbling simmer to "cook" the cranberries thoroughly.

When they are popped open and mushy, turn off heat, let cool a bit, and then start the straining process.

Place cheesecloth in a regular metal strainer placed over a bowl. Pour the warm mixture through the cheese-clothed strainer into the bowl. Let cool a little more.

Put on fresh unused kitchen prep gloves, take up the cheesecloth full of the cranberry mixture (remove the strainer from the bowl), close the cheesecloth ends up tightly, and start squeezing the mixture over the bowl. Squeeze until your heart's content!

Pour your Cranberry-Lime Simple Syrup into a clean bottle or jar, with a tight-fitting lid. It will keep in the fridge for quite a while.

For the Perry Fawcett Cocktail:

In a glass of your choice, put in desired amount of ice cubes.

Add either whiskey (Tullamore Dew is my favorite) or a silver tequila (Patron Silver is my favorite). I suppose you could use vodka (I'm not a vodka person) or gin. Of course, how much alcohol you add is up to you!

Add Ginger Ale ~ I use about a half a can for a small glass but the amount is up to you.

Add Cranberry-Lime Simple Syrup ~ I use about a jigger but the amount is up to you.

Stir gently.

Now, drink up!

The Polk Street Review Awards

2020 Theme Contest winner, Grand Prize: *Sunrise*, submitted by Deborah Petersen

2020 Award of Merit (Best in Book): *The Name Game* by Bonita Cox Searle

2020 Prose Category:

First Prize: *The Night Bobby Came to the Mall* by Sandy Stewart

Second Prize: *Blowing Things Up* by Mark Wilkinson

Third Prize: *The Pivot* by Vivianne Belle

Honorable Mention: *"Zombies Can't Open Doors"* by Michelle (Meesh) Payne

2020 Poetry/Song Lyrics Category:

First Prize: *The First Dawn* by George Wolfe

Second Prize: *Garage Sale Blues* by Steve VandeWater

Third Prize: *Tree Whispers* by Dennis White

Honorable Mention: *Good Morning* by David Allen

2020 Images Category:

First Prize: *Morse Lake Sunset After A Storm* by Sophie Doell

Second Prize: *Blue City* by Simona Buna

Third Prize: *Sunrise* by Lori Cates Hand

Honorable Mention: *Sunrise* by Tim Baker

2020 Special Award(s):

Special Award: Leslie Ober

For several years, Leslie has consistently submitted quality writings and images to this annual publication. Her paintings, writings, and photographs have been selected for a variety of TPSR awards in the past. This year, in addition to her writings and her more traditional art pieces, we love the mixed media images she submitted that are created with fabric and felt. Rather than single out any one piece, this *Special Award* honors all of Leslie's submissions of artwork and writings this year.

Special Award: Jenny Kalahar

Jenny always submits wonderful writings to TPSR, and this year is no exception. She's won TPSR awards in the past, including an *Award of Merit*. Jenny's life has been touched by losses in the past year, and we feel those losses have touched her writing in ways that many people will connect to and be comforted by. This year, as we read and considered all of her submitted poems, we decided Jenny deserves a *Special Award*.

Contributor Biographies

David Allen is a retired journalist and published poet with three books, *Type Dancing, (more)*, and *The Story So Far*, available at Amazon.com. His poems have appeared in numerous magazines and anthologies. He is the Vice President and Contest Director of the *Poetry Society of Indiana*, host of monthly *Open Mic Poetry Nights* in Anderson, a member of the *Last Stanza Poetry Association* in Elwood, and an infrequent participant in the monthly *Noble Poets* meeting in Noblesville. Visit his poetry blog at www.davidallen.nu.

Tim A. Baker has lived in Noblesville for more than 20 years. His hobbies include playing and writing music, photography, and a variety of water sports.

Arlene Barker moved to Hamilton County from her native Chicago in 1973 and has lived just north of Conner Prairie since 1978. She taught in Hamilton Southeastern Schools and worked at Conner Prairie for 12 years. After retirement, she revived her life-long interest in writing through the *Indianapolis Writing Center*. She lives in the woods with her husband, mother, and dog, Penny. Besides writing, she enjoys reading, gardening, yoga, the Cubs, and traveling to visit her children out West.

Vivianne Belle lives in Noblesville. She enjoys traveling abroad every year, usually in February and March, and occasionally putting pen to paper to write poetry and prose.

Simona F. Buna was born in Romania and arrived in the US in 2003. In her childhood she loved to draw and paint and started her first oil painting when she was 13 years old, carefully guided by her father, who was a passionate artist. Her move to the United States marked a change in her art career. She was a professional photographer for almost 10 years, and only recently rediscovered her joy of oil painting. Her favorite subjects to paint are flowers, horses, and fruits. Simona is a Juried Artist member of *Hamilton County Artists' Association*, and an artist member of Nickel Plate Arts and Oil Painters of America, and her work can be found at CCA Gallery in Carmel.

Alys Caviness-Gober is an anthropologist, artist, and writer. She taught Anthropology and Women's Studies at the university level and was a PhD candidate in Applied Linguistics until her disabilities worsened in 2009. Alys is a member of Noblesville's *Noble Poets* and the *Poetry Society of Indiana*. Her poetry has been featured in various global anthologies since the 1980s, and she's published two volumes of poetry, *Naked In Wonderland Vol. I* and *Naked In Wonderland Vol. II* (*Vol. III* is forthcoming!). She is an artist member of Nickel Plate Arts, and a Juried Artist member of the 70-year-old Fine Arts organization, the *Hamilton County Artists' Association* (HCAA), where she's juried into both photography and 2D categories. Alys and Sarah E. Morin co-founded *NICE* (*Noblesville Interdisciplinary Creativity Expo*), which is in its 6th year in 2020. In 2014, Alys founded a 501(c)(3) nonprofit arts organization called *Logan Street Sanctuary*, which rebranded in 2019 as *Community • Education • Arts, Inc.* (CEArts); she serves as the President. Alys is the driving force behind *CEArts Press*, which publishes *The Polk Street Review* and books for other authors. She is a FY2017 Indiana Arts Commission *Individual Artist Project* Grant Award recipient, for which she created a series of paintings expressing life with hidden disabilities. In 2018, she began writing film reviews as a guest contributor to *Midwest Film Journal*. Alys' artwork, photographs, prose, and poetry have received national and international recognition.

John Caviness grew up in Noblesville, graduating from Noblesville High School. He received his Bachelor of Arts in Foreign Languages (German Studies) and his Master of Science from the *Center for Communication and Information Sciences* (CICS) at Ball State University. John loves to fix problems, ease frustration, and optimize quality of life while working with technology, and he helps the company he works for and their clients thrive in the modern technological landscape. John troubleshoots technology problems large and small in industry spaces like healthcare, construction, storage, security, paper, government, machinery, food, landscaping, real estate, religious organizations, and research companies. John has been a male ally to women throughout his life, and hopes he can help both men and women work together better in the technology space.

Jess Coovert has grown up in Noblesville all of her life and recently graduated from Noblesville High School. She now attends IUPUI as a

Chemistry and Forensic Science double major while writing part time. Her poem, *Obey All Traffic Laws*, was published in the 2019 edition of *The Polk Street Review*. She is currently working on a modern urban fantasy retelling of Sir Arthur Conan Doyle's *Sherlock Holmes* stories.

W.B. (William Benjamin) Cornwell is an award-winning poet, novelist, genealogy blogger, and one half of the writing team known as Storm Sandlin. Since 2014, he has been published in over a dozen books. In 2016, he and his cousin, A.N. Williams, co-ran the campaign for Elwood, Indiana's Poetry Month. He is also a featured writer for Goodkin.org. He is currently working on a slew of writing projects, including various charity publications, loaning his voice as a co-author, and dabbling in screenplays.

Sophie Doell started playing with a camera when she was about 10 years old, and taught herself photography through trial and error, the same way she learned many things that sparked her interest in childhood. While living in the suburb of Los Angeles, California, as a teenager, Sophie was inspired to pursue landscape photography after admiring Ansel Adams' photographs of Yosemite National Park. As she grew up, she continued to pursue her interest in photography, music, and writing. She moved with her husband and 6 children from California to Carmel, IN, in 2003, and then to Noblesville in December of 2015. Sophie is a Juried Artist member in the photography category of the *Hamilton County Artists' Association*. She is currently self-employed at *Sharpest Tool Technology Services*, providing IT services to small businesses and private homes. When she's not busy fixing computers and solving network problems for her customers, she enjoys spending time with her family and friends, and pursuing artistic expression in photography, music, and writing. Her favorite vacation is to leave civilization behind for destinations in the wilderness to photograph the majestic vistas and beautiful sunsets.

Evan Dossey is Administrator of *Midwest Film Journal* (https://midwestfilmjournal.com/). Previously a staff writer for *TheFilmYap.com*, Evan has been writing film criticism in the Indianapolis area for over half a decade. He is a member of the *Indiana Film Journalists Association*. He also reviews Oreos (http://bloreog.blogspot.com/).

John Gilmore was born in Bloomington, Indiana. John's parents moved to Noblesville at the start of his 7th grade year. He has been here ever since. A longtime former employee of the Noblesville Post Office, he now spends his time playing guitar, fiddle, mandolin, writing songs, and chasing a couple of rowdy Rottweilers around his house and four acres.

Lori Cates Hand is Executive Editor for DK Publishing, where she manages English-language adaptations of its lifestyle, reference, travel, children's, and licensed books. She and her husband, Jason, have lived in Noblesville for more than 20 years and have a teenage daughter. Lori volunteers extensively in the community, including as Secretary of the NHS Choir Parent Organization and a founding member of the Noblesville Democratic Club. She has a BA in English Literature from the University of Evansville and studied at Harlaxton College in Grantham, England.

Jenny Kalahar is the author of ten books and has been published in several anthologies, in literary journals, and in her humor column in *Tails Magazine*. She and husband Patrick previously owned and operated bookshops in Michigan and Ohio, and now sell books via the internet. They are active in the poetry community of Indiana, and Jenny is the publisher of the *Poetry Society of Indiana*, the founder and leader of *Last Stanza Poetry Association*, and the president of the *Youth Poetry Society of Indiana*. She was nominated for the Indiana state Poet Laureate position and twice nominated for a Pushcart Prize in poetry. When not writing, reading, or working with old books, she loves expeditions through flea markets and playing piano and percussion.

Chuck Kellum grew up on a farm southwest of Indianapolis. As a young adult he traveled the world a bit – about twenty countries in all. He settled into a technology-related career primarily as a business applications software developer, got and stayed married, helped raise three children, and has lived in Anderson since 1984. He began writing poetry while a senior in college studying engineering. Chuck wrote about 120 poems in the course of a dozen years before getting married, but then was too busy with work and family. His writing of poems on a somewhat frequent basis resumed in 2009 after he was no longer working full time. He's been a member of the *Noble Poets* club since 2017, and currently serves as Treasurer of the *Poetry Society of Indiana*.

Marlene Million is a member of *Noble Poets*, *Poetry Society of Indiana*, and *National Fed. of State Poetry Societies, Inc*. She has been published in *The Polk Street Review*, *Tipton Poetry Journal*, *Ink to Paper*, *Poetry and Paint*, several book and anthologies. She has recently published a poetry chapbook entitled: *In Light of Joy*.

Sarah E. Morin serves as a kidwrangler at Conner Prairie, a history museum in Fishers, Indiana. She writes and performs unruly fairy tales and poems and is a regular performer at Fairyville at Nickel Plate Arts. She has published two books, *Waking Beauty (*a Christian fantasy novel based on Sleeping Beauty) and *Rapunzel the Hairbrained,* a children's picture book that forms the basis of a workshop to build girls' self-esteem. Sarah E. is the Premier Poet of *Poetry Society of Indiana*, Secretary of *Community • Education • Arts*, and co-founder of *NICE* (Noblesville Interdisciplinary Creativity Expo), which is in its 6th year in 2020. She loved the years she spent living above the Clock Shop in Noblesville, and still remains engaged in the downtown scene through *Noble Poets*. (New poets welcome – 3rd Tuesday of each month at 6:30PM at Noble Coffee and Tea Co.) When she grows up, she wants to be a child prodigy. Visit her at sarahemorin.com.

Leslie Ober is an award-winning artist working primarily in acrylics and soft pastels. She is a Juried Artist member in the photography and 2D categories of the *Hamilton County Artists' Association*. While she enjoys a wide variety of subject matter, she is most alive when creating colorful, abstract pieces. She is also a fine art photographer, specializing in newborn and child portraiture. Leslie has a degree in education from Indiana University and has been homeschooling her six children for eleven years. She is a natural teacher, who delights in sharing her work and process with those around her. Leslie is also a writer and looks forward to publishing children's books when she has a little more free time.

Michelle "Meesh" Payne lives in Noblesville, only three blocks from the iconic Town Square. She works full-time as AVP of Branding & Communications in Downtown Indy at Elements Financial, one of the area's largest credit unions. Michelle has been there for 17 years. Besides spending a lot of time working and commuting, she is raising two daughters, ages 15 & 10, and two pups, ages 7 and 9 months. Please visit her blog at www.iamnotyourmom.com for more of her essays about life as a middle-aged professional with a family and many other interests and roles and deep thoughts.

Deborah Petersen is an educator, and for decades she taught middle and high school students and was a Composition professor at some local colleges as well. She is the current President of the *Poetry Society of Indiana*, as well as a Poetry Contest judge for national and state contests. Deborah has been the editor and contributor to three poetry anthologies and was a featured poet in the *Indiana Voice Journal*. It is no secret to anyone who knows Deborah that she is the living epitome of "a Word Junkie." What first influenced Deborah as a poet were the prayers of her childhood. Later, she was influenced by the complexity and cadence of William Shakespeare's works. The most recent years have moved her with the writings of the Persian Poet and Sufi Mystic, Rumi, and by the Japanese Haiku Master, Basho. As artists, Deborah believes we are mere conduits. When she is in the moment of being a conduit, she finds herself in an omniscience, a moment of vastness and grace, a connection to a universal wisdom and discerning perception.

Jean Roberts is a retired scientist and 25-year resident of Hamilton County. Jean manages a band called *Blackberry Jam - The Folk Band*, which performs in Noblesville and central Indiana. Jean volunteers with Pioneer Village at the Indiana State Fair.

Bonita Cox Searle is an Indiana native, poet, and writer who has lived in Noblesville for 20 years. Her work has appeared in *Flying Island, Indiana Voice Journal*, and *The Polk Street Review*.

Ndaba Sibanda is a 2019 Pushcart Prize nominee, who's poems have been widely anthologized. His work is featured in *The Anthology House*, in *The New Shoots Anthology*, and in *The Van Gogh Anthology*, and A *Worldwide Anthology of One Hundred Poetic Intersections*. Some of Ndaba's works are found or forthcoming in *Page & Spine, Peeking Cat, Piker Press , SCARLET LEAF REVIEW, Universidad Complutense de Madrid, the Pangolin Review, Kalahari*

Review, Botsotso, The Ofi Press Magazine, Hawaii Pacific Review, Deltona Howl, The song is, Indian Review, Eunoia Review, JONAH magazine, Saraba Magazine, Poetry Potion, Saraba Magazine, The Borfski Press, Snippets, East Coast Literary Review, Random Poem Tree, festival-of-language and Whispering Prairie Press. Sibanda's forthcoming book *Notes, Themes, Things And Other Things: Confronting Controversies, Contradictions And Indoctrinations* was considered for *The 2019 Restless Book Prize for New Immigrant Writing in Nonfiction.* Ndaba's other forthcoming book *Cabinet Meetings: Of Big And Small Preys* was considered for *The Graywolf Press Africa Prize 2018.* Sibanda's other forthcoming books include *Timbomb, Dear Dawn And Daylight, Sometimes Seasons Come With Unseasonal Harvests, A Different Ballgame* and *The Way Forward.* Ndaba Sibanda is the author of *The Gushungo Way, Sleeping Rivers, Love O'Clock, The Dead Must Be Sobbing, Football of Fools, Cutting-edge Cache: Unsympathetic Untruth, Of the Saliva and the Tongue, When Inspiration Sings In Silence and Poetry Pharmacy.* Ndaba blogs here*: Let's Get Cracking! – Ndaba Sibanda - WordPress.com.*

Nancy Simmonds writes letters, postcards, poems, family history – all from northeastern Indiana. A board member of the *Poetry Society of Indiana*, and of *NIPOETS*, as well as a longtime member of a book group, when a pen isn't in her hand or her head in a book, Nancy designs and sews scrap quilts, plans travel adventures, and trains for road races.

John Stewart has called Noblesville home for the past 15 years. He and his family live on a 120-year-old hobby farm east of town with horses, goats, chickens, pet pigs, and numerous dogs. They also operate K-Trails Equestrian Adventures at Strawtown Koteewi Park. John is a frequent traveler, having visited 49 states and over 50 countries.

Sandy Stewart, née Thacker, moved to Noblesville in 1952 at age five, riding the "Hillbilly Highway" in the migration of southern workers to the Firestone Tire & Rubber plant. She attended grade school at historic Third Ward and First Ward schools, junior high at the old Boys & Girls Club on Conner Street, and was in the first freshman class to attend the high school built in 1961. Sandy holds a

BA from Indiana University, where she majored in fine arts with a concentration in figure sculpture. After an early career in advertising and fashion retailing in New York City and Boston, she returned to Noblesville in 1982 and embarked on a 37-year career in elder services; she is the retired Executive Director of PrimeLife Enrichment, and still serves the agency occasionally as an advisor. Sandy is a multi-media artist in painting, sculpture, decorative arts, miniatures, needlework, and costume design – or whatever strikes her fancy! She is delighted with Noblesville's transition from the sleepy little town of her childhood to an historically significant destination city, and especially proud of the role the Noblesville Preservation Alliance has played in honoring and preserving its rich history. Sandy's been an active Noblesville Preservation Alliance member for years, currently serving as President of the Board of Directors. She and husband Mike reside in Old Town in an historic home with their dog, Rumi. They enjoy walking to restaurants and festivals on the Square. Their 1889 Victorian home has been featured twice on Noblesville Preservation Alliance's annual Historic Home Tours.

Steve VandeWater has resided in Noblesville for 30 years, where he and his wife Brenda have raised three children. A decorative concrete contractor by trade, Steve has only recently begun writing and performing songs as a creative outlet. Steve's lyrics, poetry and short stories have appeared in editions of *The Polk Street Review* since 2017.

Dennis L. White is the product of Midwestern values, tempered by growing up in the 1960s. His writings reflect spiritual values, social consciousness, his love of nature, and the paradox of life. Not content to stay within the geographical boundaries of his birth state, he has interacted with other poets nationally and globally. Dennis has a particular fondness for the poets of Indiana and has celebrated the Art of Poetry at the *Poetry Society of Indiana*'s annual *Spring Flings* and *Fall Rendezvous*.

Mark Wilkinson and his wife Cathy are longtime residents of Noblesville. Mark has contributed to every edition of *The Polk Street Review*. He is an educator at Noblesville High School and is an avid fan of IndyCar racing, IU sports, and fastpitch softball.

George Wolfe is Professor Emeritus and former Director of the Ball State University *Peace and Conflict Studies*. He is the author of over 50 articles on the website *Voices of Humanity*, and three books, including his latest collection of poetry entitled: *Clapping with One Hand: Poems Inspired by Zen, Mozart and my Experience of India*. His first book, *The Spiritual Power of Nonviolence: Interfaith Understanding for a Future Without War* has been endorsed by Arun Gandhi and by Judy O'Bannon, the former First Lady of Indiana. Wolfe is also an accomplished classical saxophonist who has appeared as a soloist with the Royal Band of the Belgian Air Force, the United States Navy Band, the Saskatoon Symphony, the Chautauqua Motet Choir, the Indianapolis Children's Choir, and the Indianapolis Symphonic Band.

CEArts Press

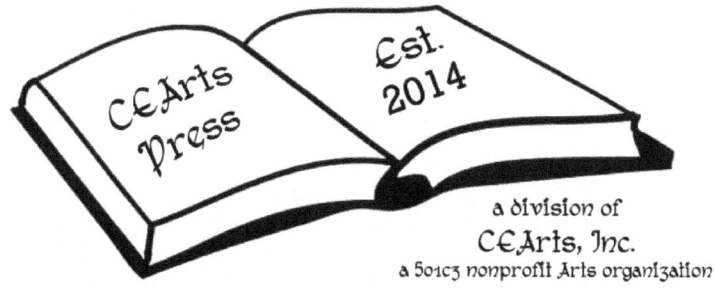

a division of
CEArts, Inc.
a 501c3 nonprofit Arts organization

The Polk Street Review is published by
Community • Education • Arts Press
a division of
Community • Education • Arts, Inc.
Noblesville, IN 46060
CEArts.org
info@cearts.org